THE
KNOWLEDGE
LINK

THE KNOWLEDGE LINK

How Firms Compete through Strategic Alliances

Joseph L. Badaracco, Jr.
Harvard Business School

HARVARD BUSINESS SCHOOL PRESS
Boston, Massachusetts

95   94   93   92   91   5   4   3   2   1

Library of Congress Cataloging-in-Publication Data

Badaracco, Joseph.
    The knowledge link : how firms compete through strategic alliances
/ Joseph L. Badaracco, Jr.
        p.   cm.
    Includes bibliographical references and index.
    ISBN 0-87584-226-7 (acid free paper) :
    1. Joint ventures—Management.   2. Competition.   3. Information
resources management.   4. Strategic planning.   I. Title.
HD62.47.B33   1991
658.1'8—dc20   90-44763
                                                              CIP

For Maria, Anna, and Luisa

Contents

Preface

In teaching about strategy and management at the Harvard Business School, I once concentrated on managers' tasks "inside" companies and on the competitors and markets "outside" companies. Other academics, managers, and consultants split up the world in the same fashion. Firms were, as one economist put it, islands of managerial coordination in a sea of market relationships. But this is an outdated view. Companies are now breaking down barriers which, like the Berlin Wall, have endured for decades. Their managers are now working in a world that consists not simply of markets and firms, but of complex relationships with a variety of other organizations.

Four years ago, when I began this study, I did not anticipate this conclusion. My plan was to understand why many U.S. companies had been forming strategic alliances such as joint ventures, supplier partnerships, and research consortia. This book examines these alliances in depth. But it goes further and presents them as the *consequences* of a deeper, potentially revolutionary change.

I have called this change the globalization of knowledge. In essence, a rapidly growing number of countries, companies, universities, and other organizations are contributing to an enormous worldwide pool of commercializable knowledge. Some of this knowledge is migratory: it moves rapidly across company and country boundaries. Other knowledge is deeply embedded in social relationships. In response, many executives are now linking their companies to other organizations in innovative ways. Thus, the focus of this book is not "the firm" as it appears in traditional books on business and economics. It is the vast, emerging, partially charted territories of knowledge-driven relationships that now tie many companies to scores of other organizations around the world.

This is an unusual topic—as a focus of scholarly effort, the subject is embryonic. Data are scarce, and many basic concepts are in flux. Only recently have scholars recognized that the complex sphere of alliances around many firms may be a full-fledged form of organization, just as important as the markets and internal activities that have been studied so carefully for decades. From a managerial perspective, too, the topic is a new one. The large-scale "strategic alliance experiment" by U.S. companies is scarcely a decade old. For these reasons, this book and the research behind it are inevitably unorthodox.

Early in my research, I realized that no single discipline, including business administration, would provide a complete perspective on the issues. Hence, I have drawn upon and synthesized ideas from scholars in several fields. Some were economists, such as Kenneth Arrow and Kenneth Boulding, who have studied the economics of knowledge; others were sociologists, such as Daniel Bell, who have studied the so-called knowledge explosion. Historians, political scientists, and some organizational theorists have studied how technology is transferred among companies, groups, or nations. Searching further afield, I drew upon ideas developed by the Oxford philosopher Gilbert Ryle and the Hungarian-born chemist and philosopher of science, Michael Polanyi. To make this research accessible to a wide range of readers, I have presented my ideas in a long interpretive essay written in ordinary English. The endnotes, however, show in detail the intellectual genealogy of ideas and findings drawn from other scholars.

This study differs from virtually all previous work on strategic alliances. Other studies typically examine a large sample of a particular kind of alliance. Such a study might examine the international joint ventures created by 50 major American companies. This is the equivalent of studying all the shortstops on a large number of baseball teams. In contrast, I examined the wide range of alliances created by just two firms, General Motors and IBM—the equivalent of studying all the players on two baseball teams. This approach provided a useful perspective on the issues I hoped to understand. I could examine how the many alliances created by GM and IBM related to one another and how each firm's particular constellation of alliances helped it, or failed to help it, achieve its long-term objectives and meet the competitive demands of its industry. I could also look at the full range of alliances from the perspective of the firm's executives and examine how they had altered and managed their boundary relationships in response to the forces of knowledge. Of course, neither GM nor IBM is a "representative" company, but the dramatic changes in their boundaries during the 1980s provided abundant evidence for developing and testing the basic ideas of this book.

This research also reflects personal and professional experiences. My thinking and writing reflect my study of philosophy at St. Louis University and Oxford University, and its unusual alliance with nine years of teaching strategy and general management at the Harvard Business School. I enjoy searching for order and coherence in the large, complicated, messy, open-ended issues that arise in firms and affect their strategic interests. I also admire writers who do this in imaginative and provocative ways, without oversimplifying the issues.

Of course, a wide-ranging subject like this one needs to have boundaries, and I have focused my research on the alliances that GM and IBM have created in the United States and in East Asia (principally Japan). These alliances are important in their own right, and they also have parallels in other American companies that faced or now face challenges from intensified competition in the United States or from across the Pacific. This focus also enabled me to draw upon some of my own experiences. During the last ten years, I have made a dozen trips to Japan and other countries in Asia to study business-government relations, to write cases about Asian companies, to teach at the Nomura School of Advanced Management in Tokyo, and to conduct interviews for this project.

The data and ideas I have synthesized in this book lead to many conclusions. Perhaps the most far-reaching is that the boundaries of U.S. companies will continue to blur, as firms create more alliances in response to the powerful, knowledge-driven forces reshaping their economic environment. Such a statement is, of course, quite broad, and its terms require clear definition. The statement also reflects the triumph of hope over experience that inspires scholars to illuminate a complicated phenomenon through a few basic ideas. The proliferation of knowledge does not explain everything. The story behind firms' changing boundaries is, inevitably, more complex, and I have tried to take account of these complexities throughout the book. But my central focus is on the ways in which knowledge is reshaping firms' boundaries, altering the work of managers, and undermining many of our familiar, deeply rooted ways of thinking about companies.

I am grateful to many people and organizations for their help with this study. I am particularly indebted to the more than 60 executives at GM, IBM, and their business partners, who provided data, observations, and ideas, and, in some cases, arranged for me to tour plants and other facilities. I cannot mention all of them, but I am particularly grateful to Barton Brown, vice president for Asian and African Operations at GM; Bernard Bryant, formerly executive director of Isuzu-Suzuki Affairs at GM; Richard Gerstner, formerly head of the Asia Pacific Group at IBM; Elmer Johnson, formerly executive vice president of GM; Maryann Keller, managing director of research at Furman Selz Mager Deitz & Bernie; Richard LeFauve, president of the Saturn Corporation; John Middlebrook, vice president for marketing and product planning at GM; Eric Mittelstadt, president of GMFanuc Robotics Corporation; Takeo Shiina, president of IBM Japan; and Kim Woo-Chong, chairman of Daewoo Corporation.

Dean John McArthur, the other senior faculty of the Harvard Business School, and its generous alumni provided me with the time and resources this work required. Many colleagues and friends provided encouragement, suggestions, and insights. I am particularly grateful to Christopher Bartlett, Richard

Ellsworth, J. Ronald Fox, Patricia O'Brien, Andrall Pearson, Thomas Piper, Howard Stevenson, Michael Yoshino, and Hugh Warren. Carliss Baldwin, Joseph Bower, Benjamin Gomes-Casseres, Richard Hackman, Thomas McCraw, Malcolm Salter, William Veghte, Richard Vietor, and David Yoffie all read one or more of the "final" versions of the manuscript and gave me many ideas that improved the book's substance, structure, and style. Finally, in many long, pleasant conversations over the past several years, Colyer Crum helped me to think through and clarify many of the ideas in this book.

The Nomura School of Advanced Management in Tokyo made invaluable contributions to my research in Japan. Under former Deans Jiro Tokuyama and Masao Okamoto and Dean Toichiro Miyakawa, the school, its staff, and the many executives who have participated in its executive programs provided me, as a faculty member, with an extraordinary window on Japanese business life. Over the years, my friend Masasuke Ide, the school's associate dean, has provided me with encouragement, ideas, and many helpful suggestions. I am also grateful to the Nomura School for introductions to analysts at the Nomura Research Institute who follow the computer and automobile industries.

From the very beginning of this project, Michael Stevenson, a business industry analyst at the Harvard Business School, helped me greatly by providing abundant but carefully targeted library research. So did Naomi Hasagawa, for a briefer period. Cynthia Mutti and Eliza Collins made many thoughtful editorial suggestions on an earlier version of the manuscript, and I am extremely grateful for all that Carol Franco, my editor at the Harvard Business School Press, contributed to this work through her persistent, intelligent questions and insightful suggestions.

Finally, I want to thank Carolyn Holland and Sally Markham who typed version after version of the manuscript. Among their many virtues is the patient, good-natured skepticism they showed each time I gave them yet another draft and said, "Once you've done this, it's finished." I am also grateful to Rose

Giacobbe and the personnel in the Word Processing Department at the Harvard Business School who helped with the typing, often on short notice in crucial moments. Their patience, intelligent queries, and attention to detail improved this work.

THE
KNOWLEDGE
LINK

Introduction

In classical economics, the sources of wealth are land, labor, and capital. For most of this century, large-scale, highly efficient manufacturing facilities have brought prosperity to firms and their shareholders. Now, another engine of wealth is at work. It takes many forms: technology, innovation, science, know-how, creativity, information. In a word, it is knowledge. In more and more industries, the most competitive firms succeed by developing, improving, protecting, and renewing knowledge, and then speeding it to market in a stream of rapidly and continually improved products or services. As knowledge-driven competition spreads and intensifies, managers and scholars will find themselves rethinking many familiar, deeply rooted assumptions about what a company is, how it should be organized, what its managers do, and how it can remain competitive.

These statements express some of the basic conclusions of this study. They are ambitious and far-reaching claims, and in order to accept them the reader must first grasp the conceptual building blocks of my argument. The best way to start is by examining the familiar assumptions about companies that are becoming outdated.

THE CITADEL PARADIGM

Most of us carry a microcosm—a small picture of reality—inside our heads. For many American managers, this picture presents firms as the rough equivalent of medieval citadels, built on high ground of heavy stone and surrounded by double or triple lines of turreted walls. In theory and in practice, many U.S. firms were, in effect, medieval fortresses in the postwar decades.[1] At their center was a sphere of managerial authority within which managers decided how and when they would react to changes outside the firm such as new capital costs, moves by competitors, government regulations, and so forth. The central sphere was defined by four kinds of organizational arrangements: administrative, financial, social, and contractual. All were ways of separating what was inside a firm from what was outside, and all helped preserve and protect managerial authority and power.

Administrative arrangements defined a firm's boundaries by clearly designating a sphere of hierarchical control. Executives at the peak of the hierarchy had formal authority over subordinates, and they exercised it through formal systems and structures. A company's organization chart showed, in effect, who was inside the firm. The firm "stopped" where hierarchical control stopped and market allocation of resources began.[2] Financial boundaries reinforced these administrative boundaries. Firms sought to own all of their crucial assets—funds, plants, equipment, and intellectual property like patents and copyrights—and relied heavily on internal cash flow for financing, thereby remaining as independent of external funding as possible. These fully owned, self-financed, and controlled assets were inside the firm.[3]

The third "wall" that often separated companies from other organizations was social. Companies were not simply formal, rational hierarchies or aggregations of isolated individuals who coordinated their efforts through what the philosopher Robert Nozick has called "capitalist acts between consenting adults."[4] Firms were also communities bound together by shared values, social norms, and a common purpose. These ties all defined social boundaries of membership and reinforced financial and hierarchical control. Loyal, dedicated employees were more likely to accept the discipline required for the efficient operation of a hierarchical organization.[5]

Finally, firms defined and protected their spheres of managerial power through classical contracting. That is, they created precise, formal, legal arrangements—usually through long and detailed contracts—that clearly specified the rights and obligations of a firm and of the parties outside it. Classical contracting is fundamentally free-market economics translated into legal arrangements: separate parties, each acting in its own self-interest, agree upon sharply defined rights and obligations.[6] Within these limits, managers can act as they see fit. Managers in the United States have relied heavily upon clear, formal, arm's-length, legally punctilious contracts to define relations with labor unions, suppliers, dealers, and franchisees.

These walls were not, of course, impermeable. The citadel metaphor highlights a common pattern and not a universal rule. Hence, it admits exceptions, and knowledge is chief among them. Knowledge flows from companies to outside groups through marketing, financial reports, patent applications, and other channels. It also flows into a firm through market research, the hiring of skilled employees, industrial research, and, of course, through prices.[7]

Though it is difficult to control knowledge, citadel-style firms attempted to do so in a variety of ways. The walls of the citadel were, in fact, intended to render crucial forms of knowledge proprietary. Executives could then deploy their firm's knowledge and skills in response to market opportunities and signals outside the company. Long-term employment for key researchers and managers helped keep their knowledge and skills inside the company. Licenses were a form of classical contracting that specified how others could use a firm's knowledge. Patents, copyrights, and other intellectual property were assets that firms owned, and their uses were controlled by the managerial hierarchies. The Japanese business scholar Hiroyuki Itami, in his study of firms' information-based assets, observed that "internalizing a critical activity is normally the best way to assure initial proprietary access to information."[8]

In the minds of many, the view of firms as citadels was normative as well as descriptive: the boundaries of firms *should* be kept sharp and clear. Since Adam Smith, basic economic theory has argued that efficiency is best served by free

markets in which independent, atomistic businesses bang against
each other like billiard balls. Until quite recently, management
theory has held that division heads and managers of strategic
business units should control the destinies of separate units within
diversified companies. In a world of atomized business units
managers can be held accountable for their actions, the rights of
property owners are preserved, resources flow to their most pro-
ductive uses, and society is protected against the economic and
political abuses that arise when firms, especially large ones, col-
lude with each other.[9] The twin principles that firms have boundaries and that these should be kept sharp are basic assumptions
in much of our ordinary thinking about firms. They are also ideas
whose time may have passed, in part, because of the proliferation
of alliances.

MULTIPLYING ALLIANCES

Alliances take many different forms. They range
from brief and informal links to arrangements so intricate that
one can hardly tell whether the organizations involved are indeed
separate. In essence, however, alliances are organizational arrangements and operating policies through which separate organizations share administrative authority, form social links, and
accept joint ownership, and in which looser, more open-ended
contractual arrangements replace highly specific, arm's-length
contracts. Such arrangements blur the boundaries of firms and
often permit knowledge to flow more easily across those boundaries. Scholars have devised many ways to describe and conceptualize the phenomena that I have called "blurred boundaries."
Two organizational theorists have written that firms resemble
primitive forms of life composed of "globular masses of proto-
plasm through which flow the fluids of their watery environment
and from which they cannot be easily distinguished."[10] Two
financial economists have written that "it makes little or no sense
to try to distinguish those things which are 'inside' the firm (or
any other organization) from things which are 'outside' of it.
There is, in a very real sense, only a multitude of complex

relationships (i.e., contracts) between firms and the legal fiction (the firm) and the owners of labor, material, and capital inputs and the consumers of output."[11] Sociologist Robert Eccles coined the term "quasifirm."[12] An economist has described the relationships between companies and their environment by comparing them to coagulating lumps in a pail of buttermilk.[13]

Abundant evidence shows how frequently alliances are blurring firms' boundaries.[14] During the 1980s, the number of domestic U.S. joint ventures increased rapidly. The greatest changes occurred in service industries such as advertising, financial services, communication systems and services, and data base development and management. Cooperation also burgeoned among manufacturers of electrical equipment, consumer electronics, computer peripherals, software, electrical components, and aerospace products. In some of these sectors, more domestic joint ventures were announced in a single year of the early 1980s than in the previous 15 or 20 years.[15] In Europe, cooperative agreements increased roughly tenfold between 1980 and 1985, and international joint ventures involving U.S. firms and overseas partners nearly doubled in the years after 1978.[16]

New cooperative arrangements have also proliferated in functional areas where they had been uncommon in the past. Before the 1980s, firms that competed on technological prowess shied away from cooperative arrangements. In the early 1980s, technical cooperation and joint research and development among European and American firms grew rapidly.[17] Many innovative financial arrangements now link small and large firms—often to support joint R&D.[18] Cooperation between universities and private companies has also proliferated, creating what has recently been called "the university-industrial complex."[19] By 1987, approximately 200 industry-university consortia were operating under the 1984 National Cooperative Research Act. Many U.S. companies had altered their human resource management policies to create more cooperative arrangements with labor unions.[20] GM's extensive collaboration with the UAW in creating the Saturn subsidiary is an example of such an arrangement. Finally, as the venture capital market expanded after the cut in capital gains taxes in 1978, and as financial entrepreneurs used hostile takeovers, LBO partnerships, and other devices more aggressively, more firms became partially owned by active outside investors. [21]

This book uses the term "alliance" to describe all of the cooperative relationships between companies and competitors, customers, suppliers, government bodies, universities, labor unions, and other organizations. This approach is by design broad and encompassing. It is not limited to links between companies nor to links that take legal forms such as joint ventures or license arrangements. A capacious definition is essential because it permits examination of the full range of organizational arrangements that can blur companies' boundaries. [22]

Consider the alliances created by GM and IBM during the 1980s. Both firms have transformed their boundaries more dramatically than perhaps any other U.S. firms. Through scores of new arrangements, they have joined forces with competitors, customers, suppliers, government agencies, universities, and labor unions. For example, in 1980, IBM Japan was a large IBM subsidiary that owned and controlled its principal assets and sold its products through its own sales force. By 1988, IBM Japan had created 17 joint ventures, set up relationships with nine leasing firms, sold products through 136 dealers, allowed 107 other companies to remarket its products, and had formed relationships with nearly 800 software and service organizations. [23] In creating a multitude of such alliances, IBM departed dramatically from its traditional management philosophies and practices. As a result of such changes, IBM and GM now stand at the center of vast, complicated, multinational confederations linking them to scores of other organizations.

The reshaping of the boundaries of GM and IBM suggests both the strength of whatever forces are driving the changes and the scope of their possible consequences. Neither company is an ordinary firm. Together, their sales represent approximately 4% of the U.S. gross national product and a much higher fraction of its high-technology economy. Their strategies and operations matter because of their vast size, their effects on regional and national economies, and because executives around the world inevitably draw lessons from what these two closely watched giants do and fail to do. Their decisions have shaped and reshaped their industries. As far back as the 1960s, computer firms said that IBM was not their competition but their environment.

As for the future, Nobel Laureate Herbert A. Simon has observed that: "In recorded history, there have been perhaps three pulses of change powerful enough to alter Man in basic ways. The introduction of agriculture . . . the Industrial Revolution . . . and the revolution in information processing technology of the computer."[24] GM, for decades the largest industrial company on earth, represents the apogee of Simon's second force. For more than half a century, it has been the most important company in what has arguably been the most important industry of this century. IBM is now the nexus of Simon's third force and may play a similar role in the next century.

Both IBM and GM now stand at historic turning points. Each made bold efforts to transform itself in the 1980s— not only through alliances but also through dramatic reorganizations, massive investments in plant, equipment, and technology, and, at GM, through major acquisitions. The price of these efforts has been high: in the 1980s, GM's market share fell nearly 10%. The next decade will show whether the recent turmoil at both companies is the death throes of aged giants or the birth pangs of newly competitive firms. In either outcome, however, their complex, blurred boundaries will have played an important role.

TRADITIONAL EXPLANATIONS

Why are so many firms creating alliances and blurring their boundaries? There are four traditional reasons why firms cooperate with other firms. First, companies sometimes seek to *cartelize* an industry, reducing competition in order to raise profits or to serve other purposes.[25]

A second reason is to *share risks*. Some projects are too large or too perilous for a single firm to handle. Collaboration cuts the risks down to manageable size. The third motive is to bring together *complementary resources*. If one firm can invent products but cannot sell them, and another can sell but not invent, they may form a joint enterprise. Finally, companies sometimes collaborate to *surmount barriers* to markets. Firms expanding overseas often find they need a local partner because of unfamiliarity with local conditions or because a host government requires it. In varying combinations, these motives lie behind many of the collaborative arrangements firms have been creating.

Why, then, go beyond them to explain boundary-blurring relationships? The answer is not that these explanations are wrong, but that they are incomplete. They concentrate on the immediate, tangible motives of individual acts of cooperation and leave many important questions unanswered.

Two of these questions are strategic. Unfortunately, the word "strategy" is now used so loosely that it is nearly meaningless. I use the word in its classic sense to describe "a company's basic long-term goals and objectives and the ways in which its managers take action and allocate resources to accomplish these goals."[26] A strategic perspective on a firm's boundary relationships does not ask only for the proximate tactical reasons why each was created. In other words, it does not simply ask whether the relationship was created to cartelize, share risks, unite complementary resources, or surmount barriers. A strategic perspective also asks about the overall pattern of a company's relationships with other organizations and the purpose of the whole constellation of relationships: How do a firm's alliances relate to each other? How do they help executives achieve fundamental long-term objectives and build a sustainable competitive advantage? Three other questions are broader. Why have companies responded to intensifying global competition in certain ways and not in others? A firm may react, for example, by investing in its own internal efforts, or by acquisitions, or by establishing new, arm's-length contractual relationships, or by creating a boundary-spanning relationship.[27] Why do firms choose loose tenuous links with other organizations and not intimate and binding ones? Are alliances a fad of the 1980s or the beginning of a permanent, perhaps profound, change in the way American companies compete?

The traditional motives for discrete acts of cooperation do not answer any of these questions adequately. Nor can a simple, single-factor line of reasoning. The answers involve forces that are at once economic, social, administrative, and political. These factors influence each other, often with changing weights in different circumstances. Nevertheless, a basic pattern emerges from the mosaic of influences. In powerful ways, knowledge-driven forces are reshaping competition, creating new problems and opportunities for firms, and leading managers to build more alliances.

THE GLOBALIZATION OF KNOWLEDGE

A development I call the "globalization of knowledge" helps explain the changing shape of the modern firm. The globalization of knowledge can be summarized in four propositions. First, there is a vast pool of potentially commercializable knowledge in the world, and it is expanding rapidly, perhaps at an accelerating pace. We now have more facts about the world, more scientific theories, more engineering know-how, more branches of knowledge, and more information about customers, costs, markets, and sources of supply than in the past. Second, a growing number of countries, companies, universities, and other organizations are contributing to this pool of knowledge.

Third, some of this knowledge is migratory. It can move very quickly and easily because it is encapsulated in formulas, designs, manuals, or books, or in pieces of machinery. If an individual or organization with the appropriate capabilities gets the formula, the book, the manual, or the machine, they can get the knowledge. (Reverse engineering is, in essence, the extraction of knowledge from a product.) Under certain conditions, which are described in Chapter 2, some knowledge can migrate with extreme rapidity; and, unlike physical goods, it can migrate in several directions at once. Fourth, some of the knowledge being created around the world is embedded knowledge, and it moves slowly. The reason is that embedded knowledge resides in relationships, usually complex social relationships. A team, a department, or a company sometimes "knows" things that none of its individual members know, and some of its knowledge cannot be fully articulated.

Migratory and embedded knowledge are ideal types: they present the essential features of two fundamentally different kinds of knowledge now driving competition among firms. In the actual, messy, empirical world, neither occurs in pure form. However, variants of both are proliferating rapidly, as more and more scientists, engineers, firms, and universities in a growing number of countries add to the stock of potentially commercializable knowledge. The rapid creation of these two forms of knowledge is a prime mover reshaping competition in many industries, creating new problems and opportunities for companies, and leading to the creation of a multitude of innovative knowledge links.

KNOWLEDGE AND ALLIANCES

Alliances are not new. Phoenician merchants set up joint ventures to limit their risks in overseas trading. Nor is knowledge-based competition a recent phenomenon: Italian city-states forbade, under pain of death, the export of knowledge about silk making. What is new are the ways in which knowledge and alliances are interacting and changing the terms of competition, the strategies of companies, and the work of managers.

Alliances are both a cause and an effect of knowledge-intensive competition. Collaboration helps firms learn from each other and thus accelerates the movement of knowledge. New competitors emerge, who often create additional alliances in order to enter new markets and quickly expand the scale of their operations. Established competitors must respond, and increasingly often in recent years they have done so by forming still more alliances—to lower costs and risks, to expand markets, and to learn or create new knowledge. Through these alliances, knowledge diffuses even further. The rivalry intensifies, and the tempest of competition blows harder and harder.

The forces of knowledge have created a new economic environment in which it is dangerous for executives to think of their firms as citadels and manage them simply as independent economic entities. This is a dramatic change from the 1950s and 1960s. Much of the world spent those decades rebuilding facilities damaged or destroyed in the war and then trying to catch up with the United States. American companies dominated most industries. Typically, they developed their products or services through autonomous, internal efforts, and they built up and renewed—again, on their own—the capabilities to create future products. [28]

By the early 1970s, however, the proliferation and migration of knowledge had created complications. The United States had successfully contributed to the rebuilding of other economies (Japan was to be an unsinkable aircraft carrier in the Far East). The industrial policies of other countries helped to protect and strengthen their domestic companies. Through licensing, joint ventures, reverse engineering, and other means knowledge migrated from the United States to these companies. Many of them combined their newly acquired knowledge with indigenous skills (such as Japan's experience with trucks, motorcycles, and small engines and its close collaboration with suppliers) and with lower labor costs, and then capitalized on liberal U.S. trade policy to build strong positions in the U.S. market.

In response, American firms began to rely more frequently upon a particular strategic alliance: the *product link*. In these arrangements, the U.S. company typically relied on an outside ally to manufacture part of its product line or to build complex components that the company had previously made for itself. The American partners in product links usually sought to secure products or components at a lower cost or with lower risk.

Their allies, in return, gained a combination of capital, know-how, and access to distribution in North America. These motives, for example, led GM, Ford, and Chrysler to make minority equity investments in three Japanese car makers in the early 1970s. In return, their Japanese allies supplied small cars, small trucks, and components.

Through product links, U.S. firms sought to follow, envelop, and sometimes shape the migration of knowledge around the world. As knowledge and skills migrated to lower-cost production sites or developed there, companies created alliances to secure access to less expensive products and components. They did not seek to learn new skills and capabilities from their partners. These were still created and managed within the citadel. But the new joint ventures and equity investments had nevertheless blurred the boundaries of the firm. The American partner was no longer an independent citadel that produced all of its own products or critical components on its own.

This phase of alliances was soon overlaid and intertwined with a second. In the 1980s, product links became more widespread as knowledge continued to migrate around the world. But many firms also began to create *knowledge links*: alliances through which a company sought to learn or jointly create new knowledge and capabilities. Like product links, knowledge links helped the partners create products or services and reduce costs and risks; these benefits were not, however, the only important characteristics of the partnerships.

Knowledge links are defined by the learning and creation of knowledge. Many of these alliances reflect the special character of embedded knowledge: it is sticky—it moves only slowly and awkwardly among organizations. For one organization to acquire knowledge embedded in the routines of another, it must form a complex, intimate relationship with it. The knowledge cannot be put in a formula or a book and then exchanged for cash. Similarly, if two companies want to create new capabilities by combining their knowledge and skills in a unique way, they must create knowledge links to enable personnel from both firms to work together closely. Finally, knowledge links often unite companies with partners that are not companies. Labor organizations, universities, and government bodies can help a company build up specialized capabilities. Product links generally involve companies as partners because firms can provide components or products.

THE CITY-STATE PARADIGM

In a world of strategic alliances, the idea of a firm as a medieval fortress that invents, owns, controls, and finances all of its critical assets has faded. A better image for many companies today is the Renaissance Italian city-state. These tiny sovereign bodies evolved and prospered in turbulent, dangerous, confusing times. Their boundaries were open and porous. Artists like Leonardo da Vinci moved among the city-states; the Crusaders and merchants brought immigrants, goods, and ideas from the Christian and Muslim worlds; and Milan, Venice, Florence, and other city-states competed and cooperated with each other, often at the same time. The leaders of city-states such as the Medici of Florence raised diplomacy to a high art as they forged and managed a complex, changing network of strategic alliances. [29]

If we imagine that firms resemble city-states, a new perspective emerges. In this view, a company no longer has a vested interest in building up barriers that protect it from the outside world. Instead its strength lies in its openness to ideas from outside. Knowledge has become the currency of modern economic competition, and a company must seek to acquire it through every means possible. This knowledge, as Chapter 4 will show, resides not only in patents, formulas, file cabinets, computer chips, and the minds of individuals, but also in complex social relationships.

The *core of a firm*, like that of a Renaissance city-state, is a dense web of long-standing relationships. Ownership, hierarchical control, management power, and social bonds of membership, loyalty, and shared purpose reinforce each other.

Most important, in an age of rapidly proliferating knowledge, the central domain is a social network that absorbs, creates, stores, transforms, buys, sells, and communicates knowledge. Its stronghold is the knowledge embedded in a dense web of social, economic, contractual, and administrative relationships.[30] No sharp boundaries, however, separate this core from a firm's environment. It is not a medieval citadel surrounded by high walls; nor does it invent, own, and control all the assets for the knowledge that it requires.

As a result, firms are enmeshed in a *sphere of alliances* that link them with other organizations. Consider, for example, a typical joint venture. Its parents own its assets jointly. The venture reports to two administrative hierarchies, which are usually represented by a joint board of directors. Personnel from the parents work together, breaching the social boundaries of the parent firms. The contractual arrangements between the parents, while often quite detailed, do not spell out every obligation for every contingency. Finally, through the venture, knowledge and skills can pass between the parent firms.

If a company is really a modern version of a Renaissance Italian city-state, executives will face a continuous stream of unfamiliar decisions about company boundaries. Once they have chosen a strategy and decided what capabilities they will develop, they must determine which activities will be done collaboratively and which will be done alone, which of many possible partners to cooperate with, and how to structure and manage the collaboration. Moreover, executives must rethink basic assumptions about strategy, acknowledging that successful strategies depend upon learning, creating, adapting, and commercializing knowledge and skills. Strategic decisions, as a result, are not only choices about the allocation of resources, but also about what a company will learn, what core skills it will build, and the extent to which it will do so on its own or through alliances.

Executives also face a new task: managing the boundaries of their firms. This involves deciding which operations a firm will perform through alliances, who the partners will be, and how the alliances will be structured, as well as how a firm's whole pattern of alliances help it achieve its strategic goals. These boundary decisions and their implementation can either block the movement of knowledge or accelerate it. The dynamics of knowledge exert powerful pressures for open, permeable boundaries. Relationships with other organizations that successfully transfer or create knowledge depend, in large part, on genuinely open communication. This can, however, make firms more vulnerable. Today's ally can easily become tomorrow's adversary, exploiting what it learned from yesterday's relationship. This is particularly true of product links, since they often ally a firm with actual or potential competitors.

Amidst all these changes, we no longer discern our familiar economic terrain, a fairly stable world, tidily divided into separate firms, separate organizations, and separate industries. Instead, there is an elaborate lattice of ties among organizations, some tight, some loose, in which more and more commercializable knowledge is being created in more and more organizations. The complex boundaries around many firms are a form of organization that can help companies remain competitive in this volatile and unfamiliar world.

CHAPTER 1

The Globalization
of Knowledge

Using knowledge to explain economic or social changes, as this study does, is a perilous exercise. Consider, for example, the "knowledge revolution." Since 1950, scholars and other writers have invented scores of terms for the societal watershed caused by the forces of knowledge. They have identified the global village, the technotronic era, the information economy, the network nation, the telematic society, the third wave, and the second industrial divide.[1] All these are ways of conceptualizing some recent dramatic transformation in the way we live, think, and work. But what should one make of the following statement?

Our knowledge of the properties and laws of physical objects shows no sign of approaching its ultimate boundaries: it is advancing more rapidly, and in a greater number of directions at once, than in any previous age or generation, and affording such frequent glimpses of unexplored fields beyond, as to justify the belief that our acquaintance with nature is still almost in its infancy.[2]

This passage was written by John Stuart Mill in 1848. In like fashion, a thirteenth-century sociologist would have noticed an extraordinary explosion of theological knowledge–society's most valued knowledge at the time–in the work of Saint Thomas Aquinas, William of Ockham, Maimonides, and others.

Clearly, the tendency to rhapsodize about knowledge-driven societal revolutions must be curbed. But what can then be said
with confidence about the role of knowledge—or, more precisely,
its "globalization"—in the reshaping of company boundaries?

The notion of globalization came into common use
during the 1980s. It represents a cluster of ideas, not a single,
precise notion. Most broadly, globalization refers to a rethinking
of traditional perspectives that reveals the world economy as a
single market, unimpeded by national boundaries. Somewhat
more precisely, the term can mean that consumer preferences
in many countries are converging, so that companies can market
the same product with similar advertising campaigns in different
countries, rather than customizing products and marketing for
each country. Capital markets are said to be global in the sense
that funds flow around the world, 24 hours a day, in pursuit of
the highest risk-adjusted returns. Manufacturing is described as
global when a firm sources raw materials in one country, makes
components from them in others, buys additional components
elsewhere, and assembles final products in still another country—
all on the basis of complex assessments of costs, logistics, national
government policy, and other factors. So-called global companies
manage their sourcing, assembly, inventories, finance, and marketing as an integrated worldwide system, not as a confederation
of separate, single-country companies.[3]

But what about knowledge? In what sense is knowledge undergoing globalization? Answering these questions is
tricky because knowledge—unlike automotive components or financial assets—is a peculiar commodity. A person who gives a
thing to someone else has it no longer; a person who transmits
knowledge has it still. In addition, someone who uses knowledge
does not use it up in the way money or inventory can be used
up. Knowledge is a social product, the result of interactions
among people, and is not stamped out by presses or put together
on assembly lines.

Knowledge takes so many different forms that there
is no simple measure for determining how much of it exists at
any one time or how much has moved across national boundaries.

Counting the number of patents would seem, for example, to be a practical and valid approach, yet it breeds controversy among the economists who study R&D activity. Some of them have found a steady and surprising trend: In the United States, the number of patents applied for and the number granted *declined* between the late 1960s and the late 1970s, per dollar of R&D spending and per scientist and engineer. The decrease could mean that we are actually creating less knowledge or that the opportunities for further discovery are being exhausted. Or, it may mean that the propensity to patent is falling because firms find that patents offer them less and less protection. They may be relying instead on marketing and the advantages of being first to commercialize an innovation.[4] In view of such difficulties, the economist Kenneth Boulding has suggested that the quantity of knowledge should ideally be measured in "wits"—a parallel to computer storage measured in bits.[5]

Nor is knowledge a homogeneous good. Efforts to distinguish different kinds of knowledge have produced a variety of overlapping, often confusing categories: concrete versus abstract, scientific versus historical, intellectual versus mundane, and so forth. Efforts to be precise can be frustrating. The economist Fritz Machlup has asked whether "if knowledge means both what we know and our state of knowing it, we might have to say that we 'have knowledge of much knowledge.' Do we also have knowledge that we have knowledge of much knowledge?"[6] One economist, after considering the difficulties of defining, categorizing, and measuring knowledge, felt that the effort led into a philosophical morass from which, as David Hume suggested, the only escape was to climb out, clean oneself off, go home, have a good dinner, and forget all about philosophy.[7]

Yet, no one is comfortable simply walking away from these issues. The sense that there is more knowledge today—a qualitative judgment rather than a strictly quantifiable one—and the sense that this matters significantly, perhaps profoundly, is difficult to escape. The sociologist Daniel Bell observed that the preface to the 11th Edition of the *Encyclopedia Britannica* says: "The earliest editions of the *Encyclopedia Britannica* . . . like

all their predecessors . . . had been put together by one or two
men who were still able to take the whole of human knowledge
for their products. It was with the Third Edition that the plan of
drawing upon specialist learning was first adopted."[8] Today, editions of the *Britannica* are prepared by tens of thousands of
experts. As many books were published between 1950 and 1975
as in the five hundred years after the invention of the printing
press.[9] In a mere two years, between 1986 and 1988, superconductivity—the ability of certain materials to lose all resistance
to electric current under conditions of extreme cold, a decades-
old, little-known scientific curiosity—gave rise to a worldwide
complex of researchers generating hundreds of articles and thousands of patents.[10]

      We may never fully resolve the vexing philosophical
issues that surround the definition of knowledge, but statistics
such as these suggest that we are, indeed, living through a "knowledge revolution." The rest of this chapter provides evidence for
the following two propositions: first, that a vast pool of potentially
commercializable knowledge exists and is growing larger; and
second, that more countries, companies, and universities than
ever before are contributing to this pool. Even though many
people accept these propositions intuitively, they still require support. One reason is that skeptics remain. They point to observations like John Stuart Mill's at the start of this chapter or say,
"Think of all the dramatic advances in knowledge—electricity,
autos, modern chemistry—that took place during my grand-
parents' lives." But even if there were no skeptics, a widely accepted intuition that there is now more knowledge in the world
would remain only that, an intuition, and a weak foundation
upon which to build an argument.

A VAST POOL OF KNOWLEDGE

      Exhibit 1-1 displays the essence of the first propo-
sition. The vertical axis measures the total stock of knowledge at
any time, and the horizontal axis measures the passage of time

Exhibit 1-1
The Accumulation of Knowledge

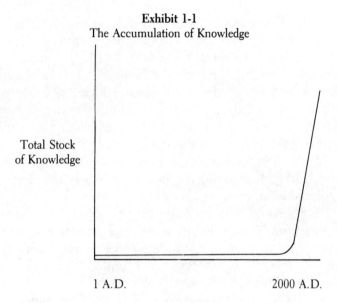

Total Stock
of Knowledge

1 A.D.　　　　　　　　　　　　　　2000 A.D.

during the past 2,000 years. Considering what this diagram pur-
ports to represent—the accumulation of all human knowledge
over all of human history—it is confoundedly simple. What does
it imply, and not imply?

Above all, the exhibit shows that the stock of knowledge has grown steadily in recent years. What is relevant for firms
is that we now have more facts about the world, more scientific
theories, more engineering know-how, more branches of knowledge, and more information about customers, costs, markets, and
sources of supply than in the not-too-distant past. Just as important, the stock of knowledge is likely to grow much greater in the
near future. In addition, Exhibit 1-1 displays a qualitative, not
quantitative, judgment about the body of knowledge and its
growth. It does not pretend to measure the stock of human knowledge in a precise way. Nor does it suggest that in a particular
year human knowledge began to accumulate more quickly. It
suggests only that at a recent point—recent against the passage
of 2,000 years—the stock of human knowledge became quite
large and that it will continue to increase.

The exhibit treats knowledge capaciously. It includes wisdom, science, engineering know-how, market intelligence, literature, and even sports trivia—the sum of the truths, principles, ideas, and information the human race has acquired. It therefore includes all the forms of knowledge that firms create and deploy: knowledge that can be sold or used to modify current products or create new ones, change production processes, or alter the way executives manage a firm.[11]

Exhibit 1-1 also depicts the accumulation of commercializ*able*, not commercializ*ed*, knowledge. The difference is crucial. Commercialized knowledge has been transformed into products, services, or technology, thereby increasing productivity; commercializable knowledge has not. The gap between these two kinds of knowledge leads optimists to conclude that a burgeoning range of scientific, technological, and commercial breakthroughs lies at hand. In response, skeptics observe that more information is not necessarily better, or even more useful, information. T.S. Eliot anticipated this debate more than a half a century ago, in a poem that asked, "Where is the wisdom we have lost in knowledge? Where is the knowledge we have lost in information?"[12] The accumulation of knowledge could pass the point of diminishing returns: physicist Robert Oppenheimer, one of the fathers of U.S. nuclear weapon development, once commented that "we need new knowledge like a hole in the head."

Finally, Exhibit 1-1 makes no implicit judgments about any of the broad, controversial propositions that have described the role of knowledge in the creation of a postindustrial society. It does not show any discontinuities in the curve representing the stock of human knowledge, and thus it avoids the question of when knowledge started to proliferate. If one cannot resist selecting a point in history at which an epochal transformation began, the eighteenth century is a strong candidate. In France, the Enlightenment began strengthening faith in rational analysis while sapping the force of religious dogma. In terms of technology, the beginning of the Industrial Revolution in Great Britain during that century is at least as strong a candidate as the end of World War II or the invention of the computer. The technological driving force was the shift from animate to inanimate sources of power. The historian David Landes has observed:

> It is precisely the availability of inanimate sources of power that has enabled man to transcend the limitations of biology and increase his productivity 100 times over. . . . to approach the subject from a different angle—in 1870 the capacity of Great Britain's steam-engines was about four million horsepower, equivalent to the power that could be generated by six million horses or 40 million men. If we assume the same patterns of food consumption as prevailed in the eighteenth century, this many men would have eaten some 320 million bushels of wheat a year—more than three times the annual output of the entire United Kingdom in 1867 to 1871. . . . One can imagine an industrial world compelled to depend exclusively on animal engines for work, a world swarming with so many men and beasts that every inch of the earth's surface, including mountain, desert, and icy tundra, would not suffice to feed them.[13]

Similarly, the technology for storing, communicating, and retrieving information was launched on its trajectory well over 100 years ago. The origins of photography and telegraphy lie in the 1830s, of rotary power printing in the 1840s. The typewriter, the transatlantic cable, and the telephone were developed in the 1860s and 1870s. Wireless telegraphy, magnetic tape recording, and radio appeared around the turn of the century.[14] Computers and telecommunications have, of course, helped firms exercise levels of control over worldwide operations that were impossible a few decades ago. Late in the last century, however, the telegraph had a similar effect, facilitating control of transcontinental railways. The Industrial Revolution also changed human consciousness in ways far more profound than recent technological developments have done. Imagine the astonishment that a seventeenth-century man or woman, whose entire life had been spent within a few miles of a small rural village, would feel if transported to the center of London two centuries later. Crowds, steam engines, a cornucopia of material goods, and factories would form a bewildering swirl. Even the humblest details of life were altered unrecognizably. By the end of the nineteenth century, time and labor were measured in the precise increments of minutes and hours, rather than the slow, indefinite, but deeply familiar, shifts of the sun, moon, and seasons.

Even though it avoids these issues, Exhibit 1-1's basic assertion is still controversial enough to require support. How strong is the evidence that the stock of commercializable human knowledge has, in fact, grown in the way it suggests? The convincing proof is that more researchers are working with more resources than in the past. Approximately 80% to 90% of all the scientists and engineers who have ever lived and worked are now living and working. Their number is likely to double by the end of this century or early in the next one.[15] Between 1964 and 1980, the number of researchers in Japan increased by a factor of 2.6; in the Soviet Union and West Germany, the number doubled; and in the United States and France, the number increased by about 1.3. These scientists and engineers start their work with the theories, discoveries, and inventions of their predecessors, and they seek to extend them further, supported by rapidly expanding expenditures for research and development. This trend has been underway for decades. Between 1965 and 1980, R&D expenditures tripled in Japan, West Germany, and the Soviet Union, rose by 50% in France, by a third in the United States, and by 25% in Britain (all in inflation-adjusted terms).

Studies by scholars in the emerging fields of bibliometry and scientometry have attempted to measure these trends and to put them in historical perspective. Their analyses of the growth rates of scientific journals, books, papers, and abstracts show them all doubling in quantity every fifteen years for the past two centuries. In other words, the growth rate is exponential.

There were roughly 100 scientific journals in 1800, about 1,000 by mid-century, and roughly 10,000 in 1900. Writing in 1975, one scholar noted that "according to the *World List of Scientific Periodicals*, a tome larger than any family bible, we are now well on the way to the next milestone of a hundred thousand such journals."[16] Exponential growth cannot, of course, continue indefinitely. If it did, the earth's surface would eventually be covered by a rapidly thickening layer of scientific journals supporting a dense crowd of scientists and their word processors. Nevertheless, this trend provides partial confirmation of the growth in knowledge suggested by Exhibit 1-1.

In recent decades, business has been a driving force behind this trend, and firms have invested heavily in resources for a growing number of scientists. Between 1970 and 1984, U.S. firms tripled their expenditures per scientist or engineer in chemicals, machinery, automobiles, and electrical equipment.[17] These efforts were driven by powerful forces: intellectual curiosity, entrepreneurial efforts by scientists and engineers who hoped that their breakthroughs would help them create the next Apple Computer or Genentech, competition among firms to introduce the latest technology, and competition among nations to build national pools of R&D capability.

These efforts and expenditures create not only more, but also increasingly specialized, knowledge. The *National Register of Scientific and Technical Personnel* listed 54 scientific specialties after World War II. Twenty years later, it listed 900. Some were the result of increasingly fine distinctions in established fields, but others reflected the creation of new specialties.[18] Knowledge proliferates further when scientists and engineers combine branches of knowledge and their theories and technologies in what is called "fusion type R&D."[19] One branch of theory illuminates another, spurs further investigations, or motivates a search for a broader theory that accounts for the phenomenon in findings of both branches.

Fusion often produces new technologies and products. The scientific genealogy of the videotape recorder shows that it descended from advances in magnetic theory, electronics, magnetic recording, frequency modulation, control theory, chemistry, and materials science. Firms around the world are trying to combine the most recent breakthroughs in superconductivity with emerging technologies for manufacturing microchips, in order to produce new generations of chips that will conduct electricity without resistance. The first efforts failed because the superconducting ceramic had to be heated to such high temperatures (to be deposited on the silicon chip's surface) that it mixed with the silicon and ruined its superconducting properties. So researchers turned to another branch of knowledge, crystallography, for techniques that enabled them to deposit the superconductor on the surface of a substance that does not mix with silicon at high temperatures.[20] In materials science, the number of possible combinations is staggering. Eighty different metals are now known to exist. If scientists searching for new "super materials" want to combine three metals into new alloys, they face more than 80,000 combinations. If they combine six metals, more than 300 million alloy systems are possible.[21]

Just as new knowledge creates new technology, so new technology creates new knowledge. Through gene research, advanced chemical analysis, cell culture techniques, and the electron microscope, scientists can now study phenomena inaccessible in the past. Using high-speed photography, scientists can analyze photos taken with exposures lasting as briefly as 10 trillionths of a second, in order to learn more about subjects as disparate as nuclear fusion, the workings of turbine engines, or what happens when an armor-piercing bullet meets a bullet-proof shield. Moreover, scientists can create and control—virtually engineer—biochemical and molecular processes, in order to make "living skin equivalents," laboratory-grown arteries, and insulin-producing cells.[22]

Other knowledge-producing technologies are much less exotic and garner less attention. The falling cost of information technology has led to the collection of more information. The Otis Elevator Company now connects many of its elevators with a central computer facility that enables it to gather, store, and retrieve information on the elevators' performance and service needs. Less costly information technology has also made it possible to take sketchy and inaccessible information and make it clear and available. Chinese herbal medicine, for example, has been largely unknown in the West, and many of its techniques have never been investigated and evaluated by modern scientific methods. For the past five years, the Chinese Information on Medicinal Materials Computerization Project has created an information system that describes traditional Chinese medical uses of plant, animal, and mineral materials. The project's aim is to set up a computerized data bank that provides information on traditional herbal medicine as well as on modern scientific research into its properties, and to make this knowledge available to scientists and doctors around the world.[23]

Some evidence on the growth of knowledge suggests a more dramatic conclusion: that the body of knowledge is growing at an accelerating pace. Some researchers have analyzed the process of technological innovation by breaking it into separate phases and measuring the length of each phase. The stages are: an initial suggestion or discovery, a proposed theory or design concept, verification of the theory, laboratory demonstration of the concept, evaluation of alternative versions of the concept, commercial introduction or initial use of the innovation, and finally, widespread adoption. This sort of analysis leads to the conclusion that many recent innovations have been moving through these stages much more rapidly than their earlier counterparts. For example, Michael Faraday made the first observations suggesting the possibility of wireless telegraphy in 1846. Only 50 years later did Guglielmo Marconi apply for the first patent and run the first field trials. Telegraphy was introduced commercially in 1897 but did not spread widely until 20 years later. In contrast, the first generation of computers was introduced in 1946. Forty years later, the technology had advanced to a degree unthinkable at the beginning (when many observers speculated that total world demand for computers would be only 50 to 100 machines). Even though the steam engine was invented in 1708, it was nearly a century before 1,500 steam engines were in worldwide use. In contrast, 20 years after the invention of the computer, 30,000 were in use worldwide.[24]

MORE SOURCES OF KNOWLEDGE

The globalization of knowledge also means that an increasing number of countries have taken part in the process of creating new knowledge. The fraction of technological innovations made in the United States has grown smaller each year, and American economic supremacy has been overturned by Japan and other competitors.

At the end of World War II, the U.S. industrial structure was intact. Its enemies' factories, laboratories, and universities lay in ruins; many of its allies' facilities were also devastated. The United States, aided by European refugees, had won a high-technology war, in which both sides had deployed weapons unimaginable 50 or 100 years earlier, and which had culminated in the atomic bomb. Consequently, the United States produced an overwhelming proportion of the world's output of new scientific knowledge in the following decades. Even in the early 1970s, the United States produced roughly 75% of the world's new technology.[25] At IBM and GM, U.S. technological hegemony continued well into the 1960s—the period when GM's sales outstripped the gross national product of all but a handful of countries and IBM revolutionized the computer industry with its 360 Series. It is only a slight exaggeration to say that in these years GM and IBM "knew" most of what there was to know about their respective industries. And what they did not know was often known by other U.S. automobile or computer firms or was accessible through their European subsidiaries.

America was not a knowledge monopolist during the 1950s and 1960s. In computers, for example, British scientists made important advances, and Alan Turing, the British mathematician, developed theories that led to an entire generation of computer designs. But America's enormous domestic market, its strong, aggressive companies, and its vast technological capability enabled it to pull in, like a huge magnet, discoveries and inventions made elsewhere and to incorporate them into its products. In this way it was able to dominate worldwide knowledge creation in the postwar era.

During the past two decades, the era of U.S. supremacy has ended. Japanese transactions in knowledge and technology show this clearly. In the 1950s and 1960s, Japan was a technological appendage of the United States and Europe: between 1950 and 1967, it spent 100 times as much money importing licenses and technology as it did exporting them.[26] Chapter 2 will show how its postwar progress in the automobile industry depended, in part, on licensing and then learning American and European technology. To encourage progress in the computer industry the Japanese government compelled IBM to share patents and technology with fledgling Japanese computer firms or else have its business in Japan severely curtailed.

Today, Japanese companies can compete head-on with American firms in computer hardware engineering, fiber optics, integrated circuits, and advanced plastics technology. And they may soon close the gap in biotechnology and other areas.[27] In 1988, there were about 13,000 Japanese studying science or technology in America, most of them employees of Japanese companies who will return home with new knowledge and skills and use them to build the scientific and engineering capabilities of their employers.[28]

Japanese firms have also rapidly expanded spending on basic research: it now accounts for one-third of Fujitsu's R&D spending. And, since 1985, Nippon Telegraph & Telephone, Japan's largest telecommunications firm, has tripled the number of its research labs.[29] Japan's harvest from these efforts has been impressive. In 1986, the U.S. Patent Office granted 14,000 patents to Japanese nationals, compared with 38,000 for Americans. In the field of superconductivity, some U.S. companies have complained that the Japanese have applied for so many new patents that they are attempting to preempt the entire field.

A final indication of Japanese technological ascendency is the increasing importance of technological issues in trade negotiations and diplomatic strife between the two countries. In the mid-1980s, the United States compelled Japan to agree to a pact on the purchasing and pricing of computer chips; U.S. trade representatives pressed Japan to buy more U.S. supercomputers and to open its domestic telecommunications business to U.S. vendors; and, shortly after Prime Minister Takeshita took office in 1987, U.S. trade negotiators greeted him with a request for "symmetrical access" to each other's research and development efforts.

Japan has not been alone. Europe has a long tradition of outstanding basic research, and many European companies are investing in R&D at high levels, anticipating the opportunities that a single European market could create during the 1990s. Many of the world's largest companies are already based in Europe, including six of the largest 10 pharmaceutical firms and seven of the 10 biggest chemical companies. Venture capital is flowing much more heavily into smaller European firms than into their counterparts in the United States. These investments rose 25% in 1989 and reached $5.5 billion, more than twice the level in the United States.[30] European governments and companies plan to spend roughly $20 billion during the 1990s on multinational research projects in superconductors, fiber optics, information technology, and advanced manufacturing processes.

West Germany spends the same fraction of its GNP on R&D—2.9%—that Japan does; like Japan, it spends only a small fraction of its GNP on defense. Germany's prowess in basic research is growing, too. Before World War II, the German scientific community included Albert Einstein, Max Planck, and Werner Heisenberg. Hitler drove many leading scientists to the United States, and better jobs attracted many more during the postwar decades. Now talented scientists are likely to remain in Germany. In every year since 1984, West Germans have won or shared a Nobel Prize in science. Moreover, German companies have continued to expand their R&D spending—at the electronics giant Siemens, for example, it equals 10% of sales.

Even though foreign countries and foreign companies are creating an ever-increasing fraction of all the potentially commercializable knowledge produced in the world, the United States is still the world's largest single "knowledge factory." Whether it will remain so is the subject of intense debate. The U.S. position of near dominance after World War II could not have been sustained. Nations in Europe would inevitably reclaim their positions as leaders in various spheres of technological development. Moreover, because Japan, Korea, and Taiwan were friendly outposts close to the two cold war adversaries Russia and China, the United States wanted them to build up their own economic capabilities. Critics argue that the U.S. position has receded far more quickly than necessary because of deficiencies in our education system, our preference for consumption over investment, our overproduction of lawyers and underproduction of engineers, and the absence of clear national economic goals. On the other hand, the 1987 Nobel Laureate in medicine was a Japanese-born researcher at MIT, Susumu Tonegawa, who believed that aspects of Japanese culture, especially its emphasis on teamwork rather than individual creativity, were serious obstacles to Japanese success in basic research.

A broader historical perspective offers reasons to expect convergence among nations and suggests that we should view knowledge production in global rather than national terms. Statistical studies have shown that in the nineteenth and twentieth centuries, the United States experienced the same rate of growth that Europe had earlier. America was expanding into a scientific vacuum and drawing upon an accumulated stock of knowledge and technology. This suggests that the knowledge competition among nations is "like a gigantic handicap race in which the country that starts last must necessarily have the highest initial speed. . . . The handicap race of Industrial Revolutions has indeed been so well designed that it seems likely all runners will come abreast at a time not too many decades distant into the future."[31]

These speculations about the future, like the question of whether or not information technology has transformed society, are not part of the foundation of this book's argument. What matters for this study and for firms and their managers is the mass of evidence indicating that other countries are producing an increasing fraction of the world's rapidly growing output of knowledge. But this trend is only part of the globalization of knowledge. How and why this knowledge moves across national borders also requires careful analysis.

CHAPTER 2

Migratory Knowledge

Whether they know it or not, American car buyers now choose among four different types of automobiles. Some are buying genuinely *foreign foreign* cars such as a Toyota assembled from Japanese components in Toyota City and exported to the United States. A few are buying genuinely *domestic domestic* cars, made from American parts and assembled in the United States. These vehicles are an endangered industrial species that the U.S. government has sought to protect. The other two choices are hybrids. Customers can buy a *foreign domestic* car such as the Pontiac LeMans. It is domestic in that it has a GM nameplate, and it is sold through the Pontiac dealer network. But the car is also foreign. It is manufactured by the Daewoo Motor Company, on the outskirts of Seoul, from components drawn from all over the world. The other hybrid is a *domestic foreign* car, which is assembled in the United States but by foreign companies, usually Japanese. In the computer industry, there are similar hybrids. IBM's early personal computers used so many components from overseas suppliers that they were jokingly described as imported computers. Actually, they were foreign domestic computers.

What are the implications of these mixed-breed products? Are they really GM cars or IBM computers? And what should we make of the hybrid companies that "produce" and sell them? To answer these questions, and understand why firms' boundaries are changing, one must look beyond the two introductory aspects of the globalization of knowledge: the development of a huge, worldwide pool of commercializable knowledge and the contributions of a growing number of countries to it.

What is important to understand is that some of this knowledge is migratory. It can move readily, sometimes very quickly, across national boundaries, and powerful forces are accelerating the pace at which it does so.

For knowledge to migrate quickly, four broad conditions must hold. First, the knowledge must be clearly articulated and reside in "packages." Second, a person or group must be capable of opening the package, of understanding and grasping the knowledge. Third, the person or group must have sufficient incentives to do so, and fourth, no barriers must stop them.

This chapter argues that all four conditions are being met increasingly often. Because knowledge of all kinds is proliferating rapidly, there is simply more packaged, articulated knowledge than before. More companies and nations have the capability to unpackage and extract the knowledge. An intensifying cycle of competition—a whirlwind of better, cheaper products brought to market faster and faster—is raising the incentives to grasp and exploit knowledge. At the same time, the barriers that could stop the migration of knowledge are weakening or falling.

As this happens, managers face a particular set of strategic and organizational challenges. These are not new. To some degree, knowledge has always migrated. But the challenges now are especially daunting. As knowledge is created more widely and perhaps rapidly, there is simply more commercializable knowledge available to companies and to their competitors. Firms all around the world are working, often furiously, to secure, improve, and exploit it—often through alliances. The results include hybrid products, firms with blurred boundaries, and faster, global migration of knowledge. In fact, the globalization of capital, products, and manufacturing reinforces and are reinforced by the globalization of knowledge. Entrepreneurially minded managers, at small companies or giant firms, can raise funds in global capital markets, finance the conversion of migratory knowledge into products, manufacture them in an integrated, multicountry manufacturing system, sell these products in multicountry markets, and reap economies of scale and experience from high-volume production.

Packaged, Articulated, Mobile Knowledge

Some knowledge is capable of moving quickly because it can be packaged in a formula, a design, a manual, or a book, or because it can be contained in one person's mind or incorporated in a piece of machinery. When knowledge takes this form, it can migrate, sometimes very quickly. Since knowledge, unlike physical goods, can exist in two or more places at once, it can migrate in several directions at the same time. When it does, whoever gets the formula, the book, or access to the expert or machine has the knowledge or can extract it.

Recently, for example, the founder and head of a successful money-management firm closed his business and returned $200 million to his clients. The firm depended heavily upon sophisticated mathematical techniques that he had pioneered after giving up a mathematics professorship to join Wall Street. In time, however, the firm could not replicate the returns he had achieved in the early years because, he said, "The ideas have spread, so that the lowest-cost producers can operate the thing most profitably."[1] After the investment bank Drexel Burnham Lambert declared bankruptcy, it sold its "little black book"— the computer data bases with the names of its contacts at thousands of firms and detailed histories and analyses of the work Drexel had done for these firms. In both these cases, important knowledge was tidily packaged.

Knowledge contained in designs. Examples of migratory knowledge are enormously varied, but they fall into three basic categories. The first kind, knowledge contained in designs, was the centerpiece of a controversy that gained headlines in the United States and Japan in 1982. The Federal Bureau of Investigation arrested six Japanese computer experts in California and charged them with soliciting, purchasing, and conspiring to ship proprietary IBM technology to Hitachi, one of IBM's largest Japanese rivals. The arrests resulted from a seven-month operation code-named PENGEM (Penetrate Gray Electronic Markets), which began when IBM discovered that Hitachi had acquired secret design workbooks for the next generation of IBM mainframe computers.

Hitachi is a so-called IBM-compatible manufacturer, meaning that customers who buy its equipment can then add on IBM peripherals and run IBM software. The sooner a company like Hitachi knows the design of a new IBM computer, the more quickly it can place a competing product on the market. The FBI alleged that Hitachi had offered to pay more than $500,000 for designs of the major components of a new IBM computer. Hitachi pled guilty to criminal charges and paid a $24,000 fine. As a result of a civil suit, it had to pay IBM $300 million and return all the documents it had obtained. In addition, Hitachi agreed to allow IBM to review its new product designs to ascertain whether they incorporated any proprietary IBM information.[2]

The designs contested by IBM and Hitachi were perhaps the most familiar and easy-to-understand species of migratory knowledge: formulas, engineering specifications, and designs. Some economists have described this kind of knowledge as a "book of blueprints." It is "unitized, organized in packages labeled 'all you need to know about X.' Implicit in both metaphors, and in other discussions, is the view that technological knowledge is both articulable and articulated: you can look it up. At least, you could if you had the appropriate training."[3]

Knowledge contained in machines. The second form of migratory knowledge is that contained in machines. It may seem odd, at first, to describe a machine as the equivalent of a formula, design, or blueprint. Yet machines, even simple ones, do have knowledge in the sense that they "know" how to perform certain tasks. Sophisticated machines—computers with expert system software, for example—know how to make preliminary diagnoses of diseases, evaluate geological information from oil fields, or process consumer loan applications for banks.

A machine also has knowledge in a second important sense. As economist Kenneth Boulding observed more than two decades ago, machines are "frozen knowledge."[4] This is why both reverse engineering and improvement engineering are possible. In the first case, an engineer takes a machine apart to learn how it works and, sometimes, how it was made. In the second case, engineers improve the knowledge they extract and make a better machine. In the electronics industry, it sometimes takes as little as three weeks after a new American-made product is introduced in the United States before it is copied, manufactured, and shipped back to the United States from an Asian country.

Knowledge can also be encoded in materials such as advanced plastic polymers, alloys, or pharmaceuticals. This knowledge is harder to reverse engineer than knowledge frozen in machines, but it can migrate when experts succeed in analyzing the materials and then extract their composition or, sometimes, the techniques used to produce them. A study of 48 innovations in the chemical, drug, electronics, and machinery industries found that 60% of patented innovations were imitated—legally—within four years of their introduction.[5]

The migration of knowledge through reverse engineering is by no means restricted to technology-intensive products. Many U.S. clothing retailers quickly study the latest designs, copy them or create variants, ship the "new" designs to Far East manufacturers, and have their imitation on the shelves of hundreds of stores within a few weeks.[6] On Wall Street, complex new financial instruments are often quickly copied by rivals. All the world's major automobile manufacturers buy each other's latest models and dismantle them in order to learn more about their competitors and to gain ideas for improving their own vehicles.

Knowledge contained in individual minds. The third form of migratory knowledge is stored in the minds of individuals. They take it with them when moving from job to job or from country to country. Although this practice has accelerated dramatically in recent years, it is an old one. At the beginning of the Industrial Revolution, for example, the best copies of British textile machines were made in Europe by immigrant British mechanics. Britain then passed legislation imposing fines and imprisonment to keep these skills from migrating to the Continent.[7] In Italy during the nineteenth century, disclosing or stealing the secrets of silk-spinning machinery was a crime punishable by death.

Dozens of employees have left IBM with ideas that later blossomed into companies. H. Ross Perot, the founder of Electronic Data Systems, quit IBM because it was unwilling to invest in the systems integration business he envisioned; he then turned his vision into a large, prosperous company. Gene Amdahl, a principal designer of IBM's 360 series, left the company in 1970 after it rejected his proposal for investment in new computers based on the latest large-scale circuit technology. With financing from Nixdorf, a West German manufacturer of small computers, and Fujitsu, a leading Japanese computer firm, he built Amdahl, a company that produced IBM-compatible hardware and utilized the ideas he had developed at IBM for building smaller, simpler, and faster computers.[8] By 1978, Amdahl sales exceeded $300 million, and in the 1980s its strategy continued to bring it success. At times, it offered IBM-compatible mainframe computers that were allegedly faster than IBM's own machines.[9]

The migration of engineers and scientists is a common occurrence in U.S. electronics firms. In recent years, turnover among these companies has averaged 20%, and major defections have affected AT&T, General Electric, Motorola, Fairchild, Intel, and many other firms.[10] Andrew Grove, the chairman of Intel, a major U.S. semiconductor maker, has compared Silicon Valley companies to Broadway plays:

> To put on a Broadway production, first someone puts in money, itinerant actors and actresses are assembled, and then the play opens. It either gets good reviews and a good audience and runs for a while, or it closes almost as quickly as it opens. Sooner or later all plays close, the actors and directors go on to some other play, and the theater is then used for a different play with different actors.

Most companies in Silicon Valley follow the same pattern. Only a small number of them become on-going, established concerns. The engineers simply go on to another company, maybe one just across the street.[11]

Almost all high-tech companies now require their employees to sign antidisclosure agreements and "not-to-compete" clauses to keep them from taking vital information to rival companies. But because such restrictions can be difficult and costly to enforce in court, and because various jurisdictions interpret them differently, they often fail to impede the migration of knowledge.

Other, larger movements of people and ideas are essentially unregulated. In the mid-1980s, more than 100,000 foreign students were studying at U.S. universities—including more than 20,000 from Taiwan, more than 15,000 from Korea, and more than 13,000 from Japan—many of them specializing in science and engineering.[12] When they return home, the knowledge they have acquired goes with them.

Brakes and Accelerators

How fast knowledge migrates does not depend only on its intrinsic characteristics. It also depends upon three external conditions—summarized here as capabilities, incentives, and barriers—that can either brake or accelerate its movement. As a result, the question of whether a particular piece of knowledge is migratory does not always yield a simple yes or no answer. It depends on the degree to which knowledge is influenced by these external factors.

Historians, economists, and other social scientists have studied the dissemination of knowledge for several decades. Their principal concerns have been the diffusion of innovation and the transfer of technology within multinational companies and from developed to less developed nations. Some of the studies focus on particular industries, firms, or technologies; others are wide-ranging, theoretical works.[13]

A broad conclusion has emerged from these studies: economic forces drive the spread of knowledge, while social factors can either hasten or impede it. Historian Nathan Rosenberg, writing on technological change in manufacturing, argues that "the ultimate incentives are economic in nature." However, his descriptions of the actual process of technological change and diffusion include many other factors, among them legal arrangements, social attitudes, the skills of potential users, the composition and malleability of consumer demand, and the availability of complementary technology. Rosenberg notes that "technological change is an extremely complicated social process, inherently very difficult to model."[14]

Complementary capabilities. Knowledge cannot migrate and become useful to a company unless the company has the appropriate "social software." The innovations that swept through the United States and Europe late in the nineteenth century—the Bessemer process for making steel, synthetic dye technology, interchangeable parts, refrigeration, and pasteurization—would have been stillborn unless firms had the human and financial capital to exploit them. Such capabilities now exist in an increasing number of nations, so that the fruits of one firm's R&D can be conveyed to organizations that will put the knowledge to commercial use. Of course, these capabilities are usually specific rather than generic. A state-of-the-art biotechnology lab is not the right place to reverse engineer a carburetor. A firm needs personnel who have training, experience, and equipment that will enable them to "unpackage" a particular form of knowledge. In short, its technical and managerial assets must be complementary to the knowledge it wants to secure.[15]

Complementary capabilities help explain why good imitators often make good innovators. Imitators, whether individuals or companies, have the skills to analyze a product, frequently a complex one, and understand how it works or how it was made. These same skills enable imitators to innovate and thus to develop new capabilities. Finally, imitators may not be shackled by the traditions, customer requirements, or standard operating procedures of the inventors and so are freer to create new combinations.

In the 1930s, for example, Toyota executives decided not to create links with foreign manufacturers or to acquire existing firms to build their business. Instead, they relied on Japanese experts to duplicate and improve U.S. technology. Consider this description of how Higuma Ikenaga, a Toyota design engineer, went about his work:

> Ikenaga began working on a car body design early in 1934 and used a 1934 Chrysler DeSoto, the automobile department acquired in April 1934, as a model, because he felt this had the best body lines. Ford appeared to have the strongest frame and rear axle, so he used these components, but took the front axle from a Chevrolet and added a free-floating suspension system for the axles to make sure the car would not fall over if an axle or axle shaft broke on a bumpy road. In addition, he selected a 141-inch wheelbase, in between the most common lengths for standard-sized American cars, usually either 157 or 131 inches, so he could use the same frame and chassis to make both a mid-size car and truck with a body equivalent to vehicles with 157-inch wheelbase merely by sliding the engine forward. He made some design changes in components to avoid violating patent laws and chose certain parts that patent laws no longer covered. The result was a hybrid car, finished in May 1935, that had a Chrysler body and Ford and Chevrolet parts. [16]

Such efforts can lead to a self-accelerating cycle of imitation, innovation, strengthened capabilities, and further imitation and innovation.

The ability of firms to take advantage of migratory knowledge has also grown because researchers work hard to learn from each other through specialized journals, conferences, and scrutiny of new patents, and reverse engineering. In many fields, worldwide "invisible colleges" have emerged—informal, social networks of researchers who study the same subject.[17] Recent technological developments have helped to expand these invisible colleges and to enable their members to communicate with each other. Once information has been put in computers, and once the computers are connected in a national or even worldwide network, information can flow instantly to anyone with access to the network. For example, West Germany made arrangements during 1990 to enable thousands of East German engineers and scientists to use a U.S.-based electronic mail system and data base called Dialog, which linked them with researchers in Western countries.

In short, knowledge migrates quickly when organizations or nations have the capabilities to understand, assess, manage, and deploy the knowledge. One authority on technological change has stated that "the independent technological capabilities of the countries importing technology have probably been the most important factors determining the rate and direction of technology transfer among the OECD countries."[18] Complementary capabilities may indeed be the most important of the conditions that regulate the migration of knowledge. They are not, however, in themselves a sufficient cause for migration. Two other conditions must also hold.

Incentives. Knowledge will not migrate unless some person or organization has incentives to make it do so. Economists have sought to explain the incentives propelling the movement of knowledge, particularly technology and know-how. They have long viewed the phenomenon of migration as a fact of commercial life. In his *Principles of Economics*, written nearly 100 years ago, Alfred Marshall observed that

> . . . the secrecy of business is on the whole diminishing and the most important improvements in method seldom remain secret for long after they have passed from the experimental stage. . . . Changes in

manufacture depend less on mere rules of thumb
and more on broad developments of scientific principle. . . . Many of these are made by students in pursuit of knowledge for its own sake, and are promptly
published in the general interest.[19]

In the 1960s, an overarching theory of the movement
of technology emerged. It was based on the product life cycle—
the tendency of many products to evolve through three basic
phases. In the initial phase, a small number of firms, using a
variety of methods, produce multiple versions of a product. In
the second phase, the market grows rapidly, more firms enter it,
price competition begins, and mass production becomes common. Finally, markets reach maturity, and a smaller number of
surviving firms compete on price or on careful, marketing-based
product differentiation. They manufacture products in long runs,
using stable production techniques and capital-intensive facilities.

The classic version of the product life cycle explains
the movement of knowledge across national borders in the following way: a firm in one country invents a product in its domestic
R&D facilities and produces it in its home country; when overseas
markets are sufficiently developed, it exports or licenses it; and
later, when maturity brings price competition, the company
makes the product in its overseas operations. Ultimately, overseas
production may replace home country production.[20]

Recent evidence suggests, however, that firms are
creating new pathways along which knowledge can migrate. In
the 1970s, multinational firms more and more frequently made
their initial application of new technology in their overseas operations, rather than at home. They also began developing innovations through collaboration among researchers from overseas
facilities, so that technology often migrated in reverse, from overseas to the home market. A study of 29 overseas laboratories of
U.S. firms found that in the late 1970s more than 40% of their
R&D spending resulted in technologies that were transferred to
the United States.[21]

The classic version of the product life cycle, when

coupled with the new pathways for the movement of knowledge in multinationals, clearly suggests that the migration of knowledge is accelerating. As more scientists and engineers, working with more resources, shorten product life cycles by inventing new products, companies must quicken the pace at which "old" products are moved overseas and new products are brought from overseas operations to the home market.

Intensifying competition is also making it more difficult for firms to transfer technology overseas through wholly owned subsidiaries. Until recently, multinational firms often chose this approach because it gave them greater control over the technology, reduced the costs and risks of contracting with partners, and enabled them to bundle the technology with management and capital, thereby improving returns. Now, however, governments of many nations try to avoid letting multinationals establish wholly owned subsidiaries. Instead, they play off one multinational company against its competitors, and they offer preferential treatment to firms willing to license technology to a local partner or to form a joint venture. This gives the recipients of the technology greater opportunities to learn, build their capabilities, imitate, and innovate. It also limits the control that multinational companies have over their knowledge and technology. As a result of these leaky arrangements, knowledge can migrate further and faster.[22]

Other government policies also encourage knowledge to migrate. In countries like South Korea, Taiwan, and Singapore, national industrial policies, coupled with low wage rates, encourage manufacturing and technology to migrate there. In the mid-1970s, for example, Taiwan used protection and subsidies to promote local production of capital goods such as automobile components and turbines. As a result, some of the largest exporters from Taiwan are General Electric, IBM, Hewlett-Packard, Mattel, and other U.S. and Japanese firms that were induced to manufacture there.

Countries sometimes use patent and copyright regulations as tools of industrial policy, rather than as ways of protecting basic property rights. Often, the price of admission for a company that wants to enter a national market is sharing some of its technology with local partners. In 1986, Brazil agreed to let IBM invest $70 million in a plant that would produce important components for its disk drives. The Brazilian government required IBM to make about two-thirds of the key components, some involving fairly advanced technologies, in cooperation with local parts suppliers. Through this approach, the Brazilian government hoped to improve the technical capabilities of its domestic firms.[23]

Finally, there are also cases in which companies are not the victims of leaky knowledge but its agents. They try to grow stronger and more prosperous by encouraging other companies to use their proprietary knowledge. For example, Sun Microsystems, a manufacturer of high-powered workstations with sales of over $1 billion, has licensed its hardware and software to many of its American and Japanese rivals. Sun believes this strategy will build the worldwide market for its technology, thereby increasing its own sales along with those of its rivals.

Barriers. The last condition for the migration of knowledge is that no barriers should prevent it. Language is often an obstacle. Even though English is the international scientific language, many documents and journals are published in other languages and therefore remain inaccessible. This is true, for example, of more than 10,000 Japanese technical publications. Corporate policy is another barrier. While scientists in academia or at government centers rush to publish findings, company scientists and engineers usually shroud their knowledge and technology in secrecy, thereby slowing the spread of information. Hence, it is sometimes said that reading advertisements is the best way to follow scientific breakthroughs inside companies. More important, governments often try to impede the flow of information across their boundaries. In 1987, the Reagan administration blocked Fujitsu's attempt to buy Fairchild Semiconductor, a California-based maker of memory chips. Similarly, the U.S. Defense Department has excluded foreign companies from participating in Sematech, a joint research venture aimed at improving the equipment and technology that American firms use to make semiconductors. At the same time, however, other defense-related barriers have been falling. In 1990, the U.S. Commerce Department greatly expanded the list of high-tech goods that could be exported to U.S. allies without a government license.

The government policies most clearly aimed at controlling the flow and use of commercializable knowledge are laws on patents, copyrights, and trade secrets. Their economic justification is that they protect knowledge from unfair appropriation by people who did not create it. A country without such safeguards would chronically underinvest in research and development because prospective investors would not expect to capture the full yield from their efforts.[24] Yet many firms are dissatisfied with patent and copyright protection, and they argue that the forces accelerating the movement of knowledge are much more powerful than the legal and institutional brakes on it. In 1976, for example, Polaroid filed suit against Eastman Kodak for violating its instant-photography patents. Only in 1986 did a federal court finally rule in favor of Polaroid.[25]

The problems caused when the creation of knowledge outpaces the law have intensified in recent years. As new forms of knowledge appear, firms seeking patents face delays, uncertainties, and a significant risk of incomplete protection. For example, Genentech, a pioneer in biotechnology, sought to protect its products through patents like those used by pharmaceutical firms to protect synthetic drugs. Some of its products, however, are not synthetic, but natural human proteins produced with new biotechnology techniques. An alternative for Genentech was to secure a patent on the process rather than the product, but this approach may lead to other difficulties. Often, other firms are already using the same process and will go to court to protect their right to do so. Also, a process patent may not be enough: what happens if another firm makes an identical product with a different process?

Further uncertainties arise as knowledge is created in more countries. National standards of patent and copyright protection often differ, and companies face contradictory decisions about whether a particular product is patentable. It is likely that the globalization of knowledge will prompt more institutions around the world to become involved in these issues, complicating and delaying their settlement and further impeding institutional efforts to slow the migration of knowledge. The U.S. Patent Office made many of the early decisions on patent protection for life forms, yet Congress soon began to investigate the ethical, environmental, social, and economic issues raised by the manufacture and marketing of life forms. Biotechnology companies in Europe are fearful that the European Commission, as part of its 1992 efforts, will create regulations that permit individual nations in Europe to stall Europeanwide approval for new products involving genetic modifications.[26]

To some extent, the delays, complexities, and failures of patent and copyright protection are brakes on the migration of knowledge. There is simply less knowledge that can migrate if firms cut back R&D for fear that they cannot reap the profits from it. Such a strategy is perilous, however, in a world driven by inventions, technology, and knowledge. Hence, if patents do not protect firms sufficiently, then firms must protect and exploit their proprietary knowledge by commercializing it as quickly and aggressively as possible. Indeed, some electronics firms in Silicon Valley do not file patent applications for fear of disclosing ideas and technology to competitors.[27] Such behavior, in turn, spurs other firms to clone, improve, or surpass what the first mover has done.

Small Computers

The saga of the personal computer business during the early 1980s is an extremely vivid example of the migration of knowledge. Many firms around the world had the capacity to grasp and exploit knowledge about making small computers, and others soon developed it. This happened because knowledge crucial to computer production was packaged in highly mobile units such as computer chips and components that would-be computer makers could purchase on the open market, and because other knowledge could be secured by reverse engineering. Firms and nations rushed headlong into the tumultuous personal computer arena, eager to earn profits and to secure footholds in what was widely touted as the industry of the future. This intense competition quickened the migration of knowledge about basic technology. It is worth examining not only for its own sake, but also because it has parallels in many other industries, including consumer electronics, pharmaceuticals and biotechnology, and even financial services.

In August 1981, IBM introduced its first personal computer, called the IBM Personal Computer, or PC for short.[28] In five years, hundreds of firms in the United States, Asia, and Europe were selling clones—straightforward copies—of IBM's machine. As IBM introduced more powerful versions such as the PC-XT and the PC-AT, clone makers did likewise. In 1986, 3.6 million IBM clones were sold worldwide, exceeding IBM's own PC sales by nearly one million units. Several factors encouraged the rapid migration of knowledge about the inner workings of the PC and ways to manufacture clones of it. First, the PC was an open system: anyone could write software for it. Second, its operating system was an off-the-shelf product made by the Microsoft Corporation. In addition, the PC's hardware was a collection of widely available components. After taking apart an early PC, one computer expert commented that IBM was "building with parts that mortals could get. The major surprise was that they were using chips from Earth and not from IBM."[29]

The PC used a chip called the 8088 Processor, manufactured by Intel, which other companies could buy and build clones around. Such chips are clear examples of migratory knowledge. They "know" how to perform a wide range of tasks: a crucial chip in the IBM PC was the so-called ROM-BIOS, which contains programs that make the hardware and the software work together. The chip could be bought for $10–15. Clone makers could also turn to a company like Phoenix Technologies, which made "compatibility suites," sets of five software packages that included a version of the ROM-BIOS. Another firm, Chips and

Technologies, in California, sold the semiconductors that made a personal computer work like an IBM PC, but faster and cheaper. By combining this hardware with Phoenix's software, any company—or any basement hobbyist, for that matter—could make an IBM clone.

By 1985, the IBM PC had become, in effect, an industry standard. It provided a clear, stable set of hardware and software specifications according to which others could design, build, and sell products. Hundreds of companies throughout the world did so, including large, well-established firms such as Olivetti in Italy, NEC in Japan, and Tandy in the United States. At the other end of the spectrum were scores of minuscule startups whose products included Great Wall Computers made in the People's Republic of China and "while-you-wait" machines soldered together in storefronts in Hong Kong and Taiwan.

Asian manufacturers were capable of entering the PC market because some of them had been making computer accessories such as printers and disk drives for U.S. firms since 1981. Some companies wed migratory knowledge to very cheap labor, paying, for example, $1.30 an hour to have components tested. Other firms built large automated plants: in Korea, for example, the Daewoo Group spent several hundred million dollars on the facilities where its Leading Edge computers and its components were made. The demand for clones was enormous, since their prices were often $1,000–1,500 lower than those of their IBM counterparts and since many were quite reliable. Some even worked faster than the IBM PC.

Small Cars

In certain ways, the small car story resembles the small computer story. Some knowledge in the auto industry is migratory and has been from the industry's earliest years. Karl Benz and Gottlieb Daimler built the first workable, gasoline-powered road vehicles in Germany in 1885. Eight years later, two Americans, Charles and Frank Duryea built a similar vehicle by relying on a description of Benz's car in *Scientific American*.

In 1896, the chief engineer of the Detroit Illuminating Company, Henry Ford, learned about building what he initially called a "quadricycle" from articles about European automobiles in technical magazines.[30] Roughly two decades later, knowledge about automobiles spread to the Soviet Union when Lenin agreed to import knockdown kits of Models Ts.

The auto industry is different from the computer industry, however, in a crucial respect. Until quite recently, knowledge about small cars has moved more slowly than knowledge about personal computers. For this reason, the small car story is typical of the experience of the many industries in which knowledge does migrate, but not at the feverish pace of the PC business.

Each of the four conditions that regulate the migration of knowledge helps to explain why knowledge migrates more slowly in the automobile industry. Automobiles have thousands of parts; their inner workings do not depend, as small computers do, on a core of knowledge tidily packaged in a few pieces of electronics available in a worldwide commodity market. Coordinating the supply and manufacture of these parts calls for much more sophisticated managerial capabilities. This body of knowledge and skill must be built up slowly; it cannot be secured simply by taking a car apart. Finally, while there are strong incentives to enter both the small computer and the small car business, the barriers to entering the latter in the 1980s were much higher. By then, the early movers had built powerful competitive advantages—based on scale economies, dealer networks, customer loyalty, and so forth—while the small computer business was still in its infancy. It resembled the early, freewheeling years of the U.S. auto industry, when scores of firms vied for positions in a fast-growing, fast-changing industry.

Before the successes of the major Japanese car companies in the 1970s and 1980s, the Japanese had to develop patiently a wide range of managerial, technological, and financial capabilities.[31] So did many of their suppliers. In the 1930s and 1950s, alliances with American and European firms and reverse engineering helped these companies gain crucial knowledge. Nissan entered the automobile business by importing American machinery and vehicle and engine designs and by hiring U.S. engineers to install Nissan's production facilities. (To build up its truck business in the 1920s, Nissan purchased an entire truck factory from the Graham Paige Company and moved it to Japan.) After the war, Nissan depended heavily on an alliance with Austin, an important British auto maker, for equipment, components, designs, and assembly techniques.

Toyota took a different approach, choosing to rely heavily on reverse engineering. In the 1930s, Toyota built a staff of technical experts who bought cars, parts, and manufacturing machinery from overseas firms, disassembled them and analyzed the pieces, and then found ways to reproduce, combine, and sometimes improve them. Toyota also sought outside suppliers capable of copying parts and components. After World War II, Toyota continued to shun links with overseas firms, fearing that Japanese government officials would interfere with its operations. The company embarked on its own independent development program, while continuing to utilize reverse engineering. One of Toyota's earliest products, the Toyopet SA, clearly reflected this: it resembled the offspring that might have resulted from mating a Volkswagen with a Buick. In the late 1950s and the 1960s, Japanese auto companies worked hard to modify, improve, and sometimes transform what they had learned from foreign competitors.

Recently, however, the pace of migration in the small car business has quickened and now bears a stronger resemblance to the personal computer story. Consider the case of South Korea.[32] In the early 1980s, the survival of its fledgling automobile industry was in doubt. Production volumes were low, costs high, and quality erratic. The near-collapse of the domestic economy had severely shrunk domestic demand, and overseas opportunities looked bleak. Then, through the entrepreneurship of Korean firms, changes in the nation's industrial policy, and a host of alliances between Korean companies and American and Japanese car makers, domestic manufacturers swiftly learned how to manufacture and sell competitive small cars in overseas markets. In 1985, Korea exported 65 cars to the United States. In 1986, the figure had risen to 140,000, and in the early 1990s, its exports may reach one-half million vehicles per year. Moreover, Taiwan, Thailand, and Malaysia soon tried to follow Korea's example. Even the Soviet Union, Czechoslovakia, and Poland are importing technology—through links with Fiat, Volkswagen, Suzuki, and U.S. component suppliers—and plan to expand sales in Western Europe beyond their current 2% market share.

Both IBM and GM have had to grapple with the migration of knowledge in their industries and to find solutions that would safeguard their market shares. Their responses have led them to create the hybrid products described at the beginning of this chapter and to do so, in many cases, through a form of alliance known as a product link. The next chapter analyzes product links in detail.

CHAPTER 3

Product Links

From the globalization of knowledge new competitors emerge, along with a few older firms that have gained new strength. They threaten the finances, marketing, manufacturing, corporate cultures, and strategies of established firms. In many industries, the companies deploying newly gained and newly developed knowledge were never members of the oligopolistic "gentlemen's clubs" that restrained and shaped competition in the United States in the postwar period. If the established American firms resembled professional wrestlers—aged, overweight athletes who feigned suffering as their fellow oligopolists inflicted fake blows on them—the newcomers resembled collegiate wrestlers, grittily determined and capitalizing on timing, agility, and speed. The new competitive environment was sometimes reminiscent of Thomas Hobbes's state of nature, in which life was nasty, brutish, and short.

In the past two decades, GM and IBM, two quintessentially establishment firms, have faced these challenges and responded in a variety of ways. Among them has been the creation of a particular form of alliance, which I have called a product link. Typically, these alliances are created to fill gaps in a company's product lines, often with a low-price product sold in an intensely competitive market. Sometimes, as in GM's case, companies have formed a series of such alliances in order to follow the migration of knowledge to lower-cost production sites. During the 1970s and 1980s, the partners in product links were often aggressive emerging firms seeking some combination of capital, current or old technology, and access to overseas distribution. Product links are usually structured as joint ventures,

long-term buyer-supplier relationships, or involved minority equity investments.

GM relied on product links to secure a large supply
of competitively priced, high-quality small cars. IBM used product links to enter the personal computer business in the United
States and Japan. Relying on such alliances was a major shift for
these firms: it was another instance of blurred boundaries, which
made the firms less like citadels and more like city-states. During
the postwar years, GM and IBM had produced their entire product lines without assistance. Now they were relying in part on
outside firms, and they had made arrangements to share ownership and control. Their efforts are important examples of the
challenges and opportunities created by the migration of knowledge, and they also display the advantages and hazards of using
product links as strategic weapons.

When these alliances succeed, they do more than
fill out product lines. They also help firms cut costs, reduce risks,
accelerate their products' speed to market, build flexibility, mon-
itor competitors, guide the migration of knowledge, and neutralize competitors. Many of the leading Japanese automobile
and computer firms have created product links with low-cost
manufacturers elsewhere in Asia, as a response to the appreciation
of the yen and to the migration of knowledge and skills within
the region.

But detailed analysis of the GM and IBM experiences
with product links reveals them to be limited-purpose tools. While
they are sometimes necessary and important elements in a company's strategy, product links can also be dangerously seductive.
Hazards lie behind the strong appeal of quick access to low-cost,
high-quality products. A partner that can supply a high-quality,
low-cost product or a major component is often either a competitor or a firm planning to become one. As a result, a product
link can create or strengthen an adversary. Product links can also
become substitutes for changes that companies need to make in
their core operations and alternatives to managing these operations well. Indeed, some product links are like a finger in the
dike—useful only because no one has maintained the dike or

paid attention to the rising tide. A final hazard is that many of the costs and risks of product links are indirect and longer-term, and they get short shrift from executives eager to consummate a deal today and get access to a product tomorrow.

The experiences of GM and IBM suggest that product links are neither an absolute evil nor an absolute good. The balance of benefits and drawbacks must be assessed for each alliance, and final decisions are matters of management judgment in particular situations, not of general principles. This chapter outlines the basic considerations that should be brought to these judgments. To understand product links fully, however, we must first see how the migration of knowledge affects companies.

THE CHALLENGES OF MIGRATORY KNOWLEDGE

The more quickly and widely knowledge migrates, the greater the force of what economist Joseph Schumpeter called "the perennial gale of creative destructive competition which commands a decisive cost or quality advantage and which strikes not only at the margins of the profits and the outputs of existing firms but at their foundations and their very lives."[1] When knowledge crucial to an industry has migrated to firms with lower costs, greater flexibility, or the capacity to improve the knowledge, other companies face challenges that affect activities such as finance, marketing, and manufacturing, as well as their corporate culture and strategy.

Finance

From a purely financial perspective, firms are simply bundles of assets. What matters about the assets is their capacity to earn a return and the riskiness of the return. The migration of knowledge can affect a company's finances in two fundamental ways. First, it tends to raise unit costs and lower revenues. Second, it makes a firm's profits more variable, and, hence, riskier. When knowledge migrates to firms that can produce a product more cheaply, other firms lose revenue because they then sell fewer units and often do so at lower prices. Even clones of very low quality, as IBM has learned, can do damage. In many markets, there are some customers who are so price-sensitive or so ill-informed that they will buy products of low or dubious value.

When revenues fall, the costs of making each unit may rise. Selling fewer units of a product means that a firm cannot benefit as much from economies of scale, since the fixed costs of operations must be allocated across a smaller number of units. Such economies are particularly crucial in capital-intensive industries like the auto industry. Also, a drop in sales leads companies to lower production and thus reduces the experience from which a firm can learn how to make products faster, better, and more cheaply. Finally, a firm's fixed costs will increase if the migration of knowledge compels it to make greater investments in R&D or marketing in order to introduce new products and to maintain market share in old ones.

Weakening revenues and rising costs are often accompanied by greater financial risk. If knowledge migrates quickly, oligopolistic stability and predictable profit streams are imperiled. New investments in technology or human skills can be outmoded quickly, before they earn acceptable returns. Attacks on a firm's products and markets come from many directions, sometimes unexpected ones: the quality of Japanese automobiles surprised many Americans in the early 1970s, as did the quality of some Korean semiconductor chips in the 1980s. The migration of knowledge becomes far more difficult to predict when it occurs offshore and when unfamiliar firms are working to copy, improve, or leapfrog current products and technology. Other surprises and uncertainties arise when suppliers use knowledge extracted from customers to integrate forward into customers' businesses. Some of IBM's PC competitors relied on knowledge they had gained by making disk drives, printers, and other accessories for American computer firms. Similarly, dealers can integrate backward by securing their own sources of supply and selling their own products. In the 1980s, ComputerLand and BusinessLand did so by selling Asian-built PC clones under their own names.

Marketing

The migration of knowledge often challenges a company's marketing and its customer relationships. If a competitor couples migratory knowledge about a product, such as a personal computer, with lower production costs, it can raise its margins and use the funds for advertising, warranties, building up service or dealer relationships, or for straightforward price competition that can break down loyalties to established firms. Tandy Corporation, for example, used its Asian-manufactured, IBM-compatible personal computers to open doors at companies that had dealt exclusively with IBM for years. Big corporations such as Hughes Tool, Martin-Marietta, and Burlington Northern bought clones in large quantities, even though many of them had been IBM customers for decades.

More important, the migration of knowledge and its subsequent use by a competitor can lead to a dangerous reconceptualization of a company's products. As personal computers became almost ubiquitous, they were accepted as consumer products, practically toys. Nonexperts could actually use them. This shift boded ill for IBM, which had marketed computers as powerful, extremely expensive, expert-maintained, and somewhat mysterious machines. Such transformations require companies to begin marketing to different customers: in the case of computer firms, to individual consumers and departmental users rather than to vice presidents for data processing. Old customer relationships begin to erode. Companies must develop new methods of product distribution and service because they find themselves competing in unfamiliar markets.

Manufacturing

Changes in products and markets affect, in turn, manufacturing and R&D. When knowledge migrates to firms with lower costs, older factories with established pay scales and well-worn routines quickly become uncompetitive. Job classifications, work rules, and union relations can suddenly become grievous burdens. A company must then learn to work with new

materials, different suppliers, new equipment, unfamiliar product
or process designs, and sometimes new cadres of scientific and
engineering talent—at the very time its markets and marketing
are changing and its finances are strained and uncertain. And,
as these steps "hollow out" its manufacturing operations, it can
find itself with workers, managers, and facilities it may no longer
need and acrimonious relations with labor unions and local
communities.

Culture

The migration of knowledge often places a firm's
culture under siege. It must learn to do everything more quickly—
in particular, it needs to develop products, get them to market,
and earn a profit on them before competitors pare margins to the
bone. Sometimes, a firm must simplify or radically reconfigure
its entire organization to enable it to respond more flexibly and
more economically.

Companies accustomed to leading their industries
must learn how to compete as agile followers when vital knowledge migrates elsewhere and then returns to attack them in surprising ways. When new competitors appear with much lower
cost structures, firms accustomed to large margins and a dominant
competitive position must learn to compete in businesses that
operate almost permanently with razor-thin profits. (Some Asian
makers of black and white televisions have been said to aim at
profits of 10–20¢ on each unit.) To react successfully, a firm
must make profound changes in the pervasive attitudes and values
that define its culture. In the 1950s and 1960s, for example,
Detroit car makers believed that foreign cars were poor imitations
of the real thing. Some of their executives responded to suggestions that low-cost imported cars were a serious threat by saying
that the best cheap car was a used American one. Others said
the early Japanese automobiles cost "almost as much as a car."

Career paths and incentives must also change. For
years, promising engineers at GM wanted to work in the Cadillac
division or in specialty areas, like Corvette, which made presti-

gious products with generous budgets. Persuading talented managers and technical people to work on low-budget, low-price products that fall outside a company's main operations is difficult. To work on Chevettes or Corvairs—GM cars designed to counter the small vehicle threat from Asia—was not a "fast track" job. Assignment to such branches can seem like time in a penalty box, not a promotion. When IBM entered the small computer business, it sought to overcome these problems by creating a separate entrepreneurial unit located in Boca Raton, Florida, that reported directly to IBM's senior executives and could operate outside the company's traditional norms and practices.

Strategy

The migration of knowledge creates difficult strategic problems for established firms. A firm may need to make dramatic changes not only in its corporate culture but also in its basic functional policies. Reconfigurations of this magnitude are difficult and time-consuming; they stir up questions of power, status, and accountability that can take months or years to resolve. And more important, even if a firm is capable of making rapid changes, it is often unclear just what the changes should be.

Executives are often pulled in two or more directions. In the case of small cars and small computers, neither GM nor IBM wanted to miss out on a fast-growing market—particularly because, as dominant firms, they had for decades shaped the basic trends in their industries. In addition, small cars and small computers both threatened to trigger an especially disturbing development: the firms and nations that succeeded in these intensely competitive, rapidly growing markets would probably use their profits, technology, and skills as a platform from which to attack the large car and large computer businesses, the traditional core businesses of GM and IBM. Yet established firms have strong reasons for being reluctant to enter head-on competition with firms capitalizing on migratory knowledge.

First of all, they may be unable to earn acceptable profits. Large automobiles have always been the most profitable part of GM's business. The customers who buy them want more options and can afford to pay for them; the greater variable costs of making large cars—buying extra steel, for example—are more than covered by the higher prices charged for them. Second, by aggressively entering the markets for subcompact cars or personal computers, established firms like GM and IBM inevitably help to legitimize these products. This improves their sales and thus strengthens the competitors who manufacture the products. It also leads to "cannibalization" as some buyers purchase smaller cars rather than larger ones, leaving a firm like GM with the same sales volume but substantially lower profits.

If an established firm does enter head-on competition with its challengers, even more vexing strategic issues can arise. After IBM introduced the PC and began increasing its market share, its competitors cut the prices of their products and improved them. IBM then had several unpalatable alternatives. It could compete on price like its challengers. This would help to maintain or expand its market share, but its returns on investment could be poor, even negative, and it risked diverting customers from the higher-price, more profitable small computers it had for sale. Another option was to withdraw from the "commodity" PC market and concentrate on the more sophisticated and profitable small computers. But this approach would have limited IBM's entry into the home computer and educational markets, and it could easily have been construed as a defeat for the firm, tarnishing its image and encouraging competitors to attack it even more aggressively. Finally, retreat involved the risk that, after a shake-out, a few firms would dominate the personal computer segment of the computer market and use it as a platform to attack other businesses. Another approach, aimed at securing control over prices and margins, was to redesign its personal computers and make them proprietary. But this strategy would fail if many customers—especially small businesses—decided to continue using their original IBM-compatible machines because of their investment in them and the availability of software.

These strategic issues are difficult to resolve because, taken together, they raise doubts about the notion of strategy itself. For firms with stable markets, familiar competitors, long product life cycles, and slow technological change, strategy can take the form of clear statements of fundamental objectives, accompanied by detailed plans of action that specify when and how the strategy will be translated into equipment purchases, staffing, products, and financial commitments. But when the environment is changing quickly and unpredictably—because new competitors are opportunistically or aggressively deploying newly gained or enhanced knowledge—the notion of strategy becomes hazier. It cannot be a detailed blueprint for the future. But what is a strategy in these circumstances? That question lies in the background while executives try to sort out the strategic dilemmas created by the globalization of knowledge.

ADVANTAGES AND DRAWBACKS OF PRODUCT LINKS

The efforts of GM and IBM during the 1980s show both the advantages and drawbacks of relying upon product links to respond to the competitive challenges of migratory knowledge. The managers of both companies decided that the challenges of small cars and small computers were too serious to be ignored. Neither believed it could afford to stay out of these businesses. In response, both companies created portfolios of boundary-spanning alliances with partners in North America and in Asia. To understand the complex roles of these alliances and the ways in which they reshaped both firms' boundaries, it is useful to take a helicopter view of their new relationships.

GM's principal small car alliances were linkups with four Asian car makers. The first was created in 1971 when GM paid $56 million for a 34.2% interest in Isuzu Motors Limited in Japan. At the time, Isuzu was an important manufacturer of buses and trucks in Japan, but ranked fifth in car sales. In 1981, GM bought a 5.3% interest in Suzuki, another small Japanese auto maker. And in 1983, GM startled the automotive world by announcing that it would create a 50-50 joint venture with Toyota, a major competitor. The joint venture, called NUMMI, would make approximately 200,000 cars a year at a former GM plant in California. In 1984, GM and the Daewoo Group, a giant Korean conglomerate, announced that they would jointly produce small cars for sale in Korea and overseas. During the late 1980s, GM and Fuji Heavy Industries of Japan sought to create an automotive joint venture in China, but the political unrest of 1989 and questions about supply of components led them to withdraw. However, in late 1989, GM was negotiating a joint venture in Taiwan that would produce cars for that domestic market and for export.

While these efforts garnered headlines, GM created a host of other smaller alliances.[2] It set up a joint venture with Nihon Radiator to produce components for air conditioners and bought 20% of Kyoritsu Hiparts, a wire harness maker. It established 50-50 joint ventures with Akebono Brake, the largest Japanese brake manufacturer, and with NHK Spring, a Japanese company that was the world's largest producer of automobile suspension systems. It also created a more complex set of joint ventures with Mitsui Toatsu Chemical, Mitsui Petrochemical, and Nagase & Company to market specialized automotive plastics. In Korea, GM formed joint ventures with the Daewoo Group to manufacture parts and components.

IBM's efforts in the small computer business depended upon two centers of initiative, the United States and Japan, and both efforts relied on alliances. In the United States, IBM turned to Microsoft and Intel. Microsoft, which supplied the PC's operating system, had been a partner in IBM software development throughout the 1980s. Intel, which produced the PC's microchip, was also a long-term IBM supplier. For a time, Intel had been IBM's only outside source of semiconductors, and its sales to IBM accounted for 10% to 15% of its revenues. During the mid-1980s, IBM owned 20% of Intel. (IBM's investment provided funding for Intel R&D at a time when semiconductor prices had slumped deeply.)

IBM Japan went even further than IBM USA in creating unprecedented cooperative arrangements to enter the small computer business.[3] Its counterpart to the PC was the

Multistation 5550. Like the PC, the 5550 was designed to use off-the-shelf components readily available in Japan. To provide sales coverage, IBM Japan broke a long-standing tradition by creating a third-party sales force of independent dealers. By the end of 1982, IBM Japan's 26 retail dealers included Tokyo Nissan Auto Sales, a large liquor wholesaler, a specialty paper dealer, and a fuel oil distributor. By the end of 1984, it had 75 dealers and, because many of them had branch offices and subdealers, more than 400 sales outlets. IBM Japan also created joint ventures with a trading company, with the Japan Business Computer Corporation, with Ricoh, and later with Nippon Steel, in order to sell IBM small computers and systems based on them.

IBM Japan also took another bold step. For the first time in IBM history, IBM Japan formed an agreement with an outside company to manufacture an IBM computer. Matsushita, the world's largest computer electronics company, whose products sold under the Panasonic, Quasar, and Technics brand names, produced the 5550's central computer system and its displays. In addition, IBM Japan arranged for Oki Electric to produce the 5550's printer and for Alps Electric to produce its keyboard.

The Goals of Alliances

To what extent did these alliances help IBM and GM respond to the challenges posed by the migration of knowledge? What lessons can they offer to the managers of other companies? The answer to these questions lies in the examination of each of the goals that these alliances are intended to achieve.

Reducing costs. By pursuing lower costs, both GM and IBM were responding directly to one of the most serious challenges of migratory knowledge—its tendency to create competition that drives down a firm's profits and raises its financial risks. The achievement of this goal is crucial, for the simple reason that knowledge often migrates to companies with lower costs. All else being equal, the firms with higher costs lose market share, their profit margins erode, and they have less money to

invest in advertising, distribution, human resources, and the development of new products. A company risks spiralling downward
through a vicious economic cycle.

GM's Asian alliances reduced its costs and helped it
compete more effectively in the small car business. All of GM's
alliances, except for its link with Isuzu, were created during the
early 1980s, when Japanese automobile manufacturers could de-
liver a small car to the United States at a price $1,500–2,000
less than American manufacturers could achieve. The subcompact Isuzu built for GM cost $2,857 to manufacture, nearly
$3,000 less than the S-car, the vehicle GM had initially planned
to build in the United States.[4] By making cars in Korea, GM
hoped to secure even lower costs than in Japan. In the early
1980s, the magnitude of these cost savings promised to be enormous, since the market for small cars was growing explosively.
In 1983, for example, a GM marketing executive estimated that
subcompact cars could account for 40% of the U.S. automobile
market by 1990.[5] GM's alliances gave it access to more than
500,000 cost-competitive, good- or excellent-quality small cars
a year. In round numbers, Isuzu, Suzuki, and Daewoo could
each provide 100,000 cars a year from their Asian operations.
NUMMI could produce 200,000 cars a year. A savings of $2,000
per car on one-half million cars annually amounts to roughly $1
billion in lower costs—a substantial amount by any standard and
a crucial sum in a market with cutthroat competition.

The personal computer business was also intensely
competitive in the early 1980s, and IBM's alliances provided it
with important cost advantages. Matsushita was an ideal partner
for IBM Japan: it could make the 5550 at much lower cost than
IBM Japan could; it had long experience with low-cost, high-
quality, high-volume manufacturing, which gave it economies
of scale and experience; it had invested heavily to make its manufacturing operations more efficient, largely because it faced intense competition in the consumer electronics business;
moreover, it was not a competitor in the personal computer
business and had supplied both IBM USA and IBM Japan for
many years. Similarly, by creating a third-party sales force of

independent dealers and joint venture partners, IBM acquired a network of convenient sales outlets that cost far less than its large internal sales force of mainframe marketing representatives.

Through their alliances, IBM and GM also reduced costs in several indirect ways. GM gained leverage through its portfolio of alliances. With four Asian sources of small cars and the prospect of Saturn, GM was much less dependent on any one of its Asian allies than it would have been with only one Asian partner. Reliance upon low-cost, high-caliber labor in Asia also enhanced GM's bargaining position with the UAW. Third, the availability of high-quality, Asian-made parts gave GM the option of reducing its dependence on its in-house parts suppliers and its U.S. suppliers. Because GM's and IBM's Asian partners faced intense competition in their home markets, they were continually seeking ways to lower their costs—by making their Japanese operations more efficient and by procuring components from lower-cost production sites elsewhere in Asia, through subsidiaries or their own networks of product links. Both GM and Toyota secured cost benefits from their collaboration. Although NUMMI was located in California, Toyota's vast high-volume operations and its tightly orchestrated complex of suppliers in Toyota City supplied parts and components to NUMMI, increasing Toyota City's efficiency and lowering GM's costs.

These cost advantages are not, however, straightforward gains. What matters competitively are relative costs. Thus, while GM got low-cost Novas from NUMMI, Toyota gained economies of scale and experience in Japan when it made components for the Nova. Matsushita gained similar economies in making the 5550 for IBM Japan. Managing an alliance also entails coordination costs. How high these are depends upon the scale at which the alliance operates. Suzuki, for example, had 20 people working in its "GM Department."[6] If GM had twice as many employees involved with Suzuki and if, on average, each of the sixty people involved cost their employers $150,000 a year, the total annual cost would be roughly $10 million—an amount that would be covered by the $2,000/car gross margins on sales of 5,000 cars. At low volume, these costs are crucial; at higher volumes, they are less so, but they do partially offset the cost savings of an alliance. Finally, costs rise when a firm makes changes in its operations to take advantage of an alliance. GM's creation of GEO, which sells vehicles from its Asian allies, involved not only new marketing, dealer incentives and education, and closing down existing operations, but also reorganizing part of a firm and retraining employees to enable them to deal effectively with an ally. There were, in addition, the trial and error costs of getting all these things right. If a company does not take these steps and incur their costs, its alliances can easily be treated as organizational stepchildren and their potential will remain untapped.

Reducing risk. As the first part of this chapter explained, the rapid migration of knowledge has led to the emergence of strong global competitors; it has made business considerably riskier by weakening profits, shortening life cycles, creating uncertainty about the origin of the next competitive attack, and increasing the variability of a firm's stream of income. The principal way in which alliances can help a firm reduce these risks is by enabling it to compete in businesses, like the small car and the small computer businesses, through which knowledge swirls rapidly and perilously, and yet to do so without committing the resources that would be required to create manufacturing, sales, and distribution operations or to acquire firms in the business.

GM invested "only" $1 billion to gain access to approximately 500,000 high-quality small cars a year. In contrast, car makers spend as much as $500 million to develop a single new engine and build the capacity to produce it. GM's investment was spread out over more than a decade and hence was a tiny fraction of its total cash flow in the 1980s. Indeed, the investment tied up even less of GM's capital because the Daewoo joint ventures were partially financed with funds provided by Korean banks and because its investment in NUMMI was, in part, a plant that had been shuttered. Similarly, by relying on partnerships with outside suppliers, IBM did not incur the startup costs, capital investment, and learning costs of creating its own high-volume manufacturing operations for personal computers. Nor did it need to spend money retraining a sales force to handle consumer and small business sales.

Reducing risks through alliances, however, is not simply a matter of decreasing the funds at stake in an investment. IBM's personal computer alliances enabled it to test the water in the business, to begin learning about unfamiliar customers and suppliers, about whether its ways of doing business could be changed enough to enable it to succeed, and whether the small computer business would grow in ways that made further investments profitable. If the business did not develop in the way that IBM had hoped, it was not stuck with manufacturing and distribution operations dedicated to small computers. Similarly, GM's Asian alliances served as an insurance policy against the risks that the small car market would grow explosively and that GM's Saturn subsidiary would not enable it to compete effectively in the small car business. In actuality, growth in the small car segment slowed in the mid- and late 1980s. GM, in turn, purchased fewer cars from its Asian allies, but it did not have to shut down small car manufacturing operations in North America. In contrast, if the small car market had grown as rapidly as was widely forecast in the early 1980s, GM would have been able to meet a larger demand for small car sales through its Asian affiliates.

Alliances can also let firms work together while reducing some of the risks involved in mergers. One of the major risks is that the cultures of merging companies will prevent them from working together successfully or at least involve them in a long period of turmoil. This is especially likely when the two cultures are dramatically different, a situation that arose in many of GM's partnerships with Asian companies. But this advantage, like the cost advantage, is only partial. Alliances do not eliminate cultural gaps. A Suzuki executive, for example, made these comments on dealings with GM:

The United States is a very creative society but with regard to ROI, where one has to look

into the future, particularly in the manufacturing
sector, they are too stodgy, too oriented around ROI.
Suzuki and Japanese companies look at ROI over a
short period of time and roughly three years, where
they feel ROI can be accurate, and go ahead and do
it, with a *yaruki* (can-do) spirit, and make it
work. . . . GM goes strictly by ROI.[7]

Firms can also reduce risk by creating portfolios of
alliances, as GM did in Asia. For example, GM's 1981 partnership with Suzuki reduced its dependence on Isuzu. In the early
1980s, GM urgently needed a steady, reliable supply of small
cars. On the whole, Isuzu seemed capable of helping GM meet
this need, but it was still fundamentally a truck company, its
financial position was weak, and it was having difficulty holding
on to an already small share of the intensely competitive Japanese
car market. Without the relationship with Suzuki, GM would
have been too heavily dependent upon Isuzu at a time when the
U.S. market was demanding more small cars. The GM-Toyota
venture further spread GM's risks. And, when GM allied itself
with Daewoo, its foreign exchange risks fell because Daewoo's
products were denominated in Korea's currency, the won, which
was tied to the U.S. dollar and which did not appreciate as rapidly
as the yen did in the 1980s. Finally, a range of alliances reduces
a firm's risk in the sense that if regulatory, economic, or political
problems damaged one of the allies, it could rely more heavily
on the other firms.

As these risks fall, however, others rise. The most
serious is the creation or invigoration of a competitor. Many of
IBM's and GM's allies gained, not only additional sales volume,
but technology, know-how, market access, and a better glimpse
at the operations and management of a leading firm. A GM
manager commented:

We loved to show off, so when Suzuki
would say, "gee, we'd love to come over and see how
successful you guys really are," we'd say, "sure,

come on over, we'd love to show you." We invited
them to our winter and summer testing grounds and
of course they diligently wrote their notes and observed. Eventually we woke up and realized that we
were teaching them in a few short years what it had
taken us many years to learn.[8]

Accelerating speed to market. The faster knowledge
migrates and the more aggressively competitors exploit it, the
briefer the period in which a firm can cover the fixed costs of
developing a product and earn an acceptable return on its investment. It is often not a product that has an abbreviated life
cycle, but rather a particular model of a product. In either case,
however, the window of profitability can slam shut quickly as
competitors crowd into a market, fill up dealer shelves and ware-
houses with clones or look-alikes, and exhaust the pool of potential customers.

Alliances can increase speed to market in two ways.
First, they can enable a firm to sell a product or model or service
today because its partner has the product or service immediately
available. Both IBM Japan and IBM USA needed this kind of
assistance in the early 1980s. In the United States, Apple, Tandy
(the parent of Radio Shack), and many other firms were racing
into the market for small computers. In Japan, NEC and Fujitsu
were leading the development of small machines, followed by a
host of other firms. IBM responded by selling personal computers
that relied on many off-the-shelf components, as well as on the
special strengths of its partners, such as the proven manufacturing
expertise of Matsushita or the software design skills of Microsoft.
IBM was thus able to move rapidly into the small computer
business with a high-quality product and to begin making up the
ground its late entry had cost it.

The second way in which an alliance can increase
a company's speed to market is by widening its network of distribution outlets.[9] A company can sell its products on its own,
and its partners can sell the same products. This permits a larger
volume of sales during the period, often brief, in which a com-

pany can earn a healthy return on a new product or service. IBM learned that the knowledge embodied in each successive generation of personal computers would quickly migrate into the hands of competitors, and it was thus determined to sell each of its new models as vigorously as possible. IBM Japan did this by creating joint venture partnerships and a network of dealers that could sell on a wide scale each generation of personal computers that IBM introduced. Through these cooperative arrangements, IBM could sell more of its products than by relying simply on its own internal sales force.

GM's needs were just as urgent in the early 1980s. The Iranian oil crisis of 1979 led to the evaporation of demand for standard-sized and larger American cars. By 1983, subcompact sales had tripled from their 1970 level, GM's share of these sales had been falling steadily, reaching 19% in 1983. For GM, with its preoccupation with standard-sized and larger cars and its frustrated efforts to repel sales of imports through the Corvair, the Vega, and the Chevette, this was a deeply intimidating threat. In the distant future, GM could hope that the Saturn project would enable it to produce high-quality, cost-competitive cars on its own. In the interim, however, it relied on its Asian allies to help it quickly meet the demands of the market.

GM's alliance with Suzuki was particularly important. At the time of the GM deal, Suzuki was Japan's largest manufacturer of minicars. These vehicles were so small that they failed to meet the minimum size required by safety regulations in most Western markets. However, somewhat larger versions of Suzuki's basic vehicle, large enough to meet safety regulations, were likely to sell strongly if fuel prices continued to escalate. Indeed, the vehicle that Suzuki and GM ultimately produced— the Sprint—was one of the most fuel-efficient cars sold in the United States in the 1980s.

Building flexibility. The more varied and uncertain a company's environment is, the more flexible its repertory of responses should be. Alliances enable a company to keep more irons in the fire than it could by relying on its own independent efforts or on mergers and acquisitions.

In some cases, an alliance proves to be a valuable alternative to an acquisition. Government regulations sometimes prohibit acquisitions. Japanese government regulations limited GM's investment in Isuzu to less than 50% of Isuzu's shares. U.S. antitrust rules nearly prevented GM and Toyota from creating NUMMI, and almost surely would have done so had the alliance been proposed five years earlier. Similarly, GM's joint ventures with component suppliers in Japan enabled it to work with companies that were in the Nissan group. The principal affiliation of the companies was, of course, to Nissan. They were not for sale, but through alliances GM was able to work closely with several of them, thereby gaining access to new products and technologies, some of which it felt might prove useful, depending on how the turbulent, uncertain environment in the auto industry evolved.

More important, however, the globalization of knowledge has made it difficult for companies, even ones with huge research budgets like IBM, to make significant investments in all the specialized areas of technology that could affect their businesses. In the 1980s, thousands of small new companies sprang into existence in the computer business. The vast majority concentrated upon one small segment: software, storage devices, telecommunications equipment, software for computer-aided design and engineering, controllers and fiber-optic devices that manage networks, mixed-service equipment that combines voice, data, video, imaging, and other functions, message-switching systems, modems, or the testing and measurement equipment used by the manufacturers of all the other products. Moreover, these firms often specialize in niches of one of the areas. In the 1980s, for example, more than a hundred new firms emerged in the semiconductor business, designing and manufacturing specialized circuits. A firm, of course, must invest heavily in the technological areas that are important to its future, and it can make acquisitions of firms with technology or skills that relate to its core business. But alliances enable a firm to scrutinize, experiment with, and take advantage of the products, technology, and ideas of a wider range of companies.

In spite of these advantages, product links can also render a company *less* flexible, even though a quick broadening of its product line may suggest otherwise. IBM's small computer alliances and GM's small car alliances are "parallel" organizations. They provide the firm with products it could not make itself (or could not make as cheaply, or as quickly, or at the same level of quality). In doing so, the alliances act as a buffer, reducing the pressures for a company to change its basic functional policies, long-term objectives, and ways of doing business.

Monitoring competitors. A firm's alliances can become windows through which it can observe how, when, and where its competitors are deploying newly created or recently acquired knowledge and skills.

This advantage was useful for GM in Asia. For decades, it had been primarily a North American company, with most of its sales and production taking place in the United States and Canada. Its most important overseas activities took place in West Germany and Great Britain, through two wholly owned subsidiaries, Adam Opel and Vauxhall. Before the 1970s, GM's principal activity in Asia had been its small, wholly owned Holden's subsidiary in Australia. Even by the early 1980s, GM divisions had procured few components in Japan. In 1980, when the quality and cost of Japanese cars and parts were an accepted fact of industrial life, GM was purchasing only about $100 million worth of components in Japan—namely electronics—and virtually none in Korea or elsewhere in Asia. GM also knew little about the increasingly important subcompact market.

Once it had created its network of affiliates, GM had the chance to learn more about technological developments in Asia. These ranged from the success or failure of firms like Isuzu and Suzuki, which were trying to make low-tech parts in South Asia, to the high-tech automotive electronic research of Hitachi and the robotics effort at Fanuc. Through its alliances GM also gained windows on some of its most powerful competitors. It learned more about Toyota through NUMMI, as well as by observing Toyota's behavior in the Japanese market through the eyes of its long-time domestic competitors, Suzuki and Isuzu.

For example, when GM was considering its alliance with Suzuki, it relied upon Isuzu for help in estimating Toyota's and Honda's production costs for the kind of very small vehicles that Suzuki might produce for GM. Similarly, in Korea, GM gained a deeper perspective on the efforts of Hyundai by competing directly with it through the Daewoo Motor Company. By working on projects with leading Japanese firms, GM hoped to understand and shape technological developments from the earliest stages, rather than waiting until a competitor produced a car that competed with GM vehicles and then trying to learn about the technology by reverse engineering.

At the same time, GM's alliances helped to close or at least narrow these windows for its domestic competitors. By and large, GM's major partners did not have joint ventures or major cooperative endeavors with Ford or Chrysler. Nissan had several small joint efforts with Ford, and GM's agent suppliers of parts and components supplied other overseas firms, but in the cases of Isuzu, Suzuki, Toyota, and Daewoo, GM had managed to preempt its principal competitors.

Guiding the migration of knowledge. Alliances can also help a firm reduce risk by enabling it to influence the direction in which knowledge flows and the speed at which it moves. This approach follows Charles de Gaulle's observation that good politicians "exploit the inevitable." In the case of small cars, the likelihood was high that knowledge would quickly migrate to Korea. Faced with intensifying competition in the 1980s, American and Japanese companies sought lower-cost suppliers of basic parts in a number of Asian countries, including Korea. The Korean national industrial plan further encouraged these firms to invest in the country. By the late 1970s, Mitsubishi, Toyota, American Motors, Nissan, and Mazda were among the auto makers that already had links with firms in Korea's embryonic automobile industry. GM itself had been linked with Daewoo since 1972, when it purchased a 50% share of Shinjin Industrial, a small Korean auto maker, and established a joint venture Shinjin called GM-Korea.

When the Korean automobile market seemed poised for a leap forward and opportunities for GM to sell Korean-made cars overseas seemed bright, GM acted vigorously. It did not wait for several Korean auto makers to emerge and then form alliances with one of them. Instead, it created six new joint ventures with the Daewoo Group.[10] A team of engineers from Daewoo, GM, and GM's West German subsidiary Adam Opel collaborated to plan the Daewoo Motor Company. The plant they devised used state-of-the-art technology, such as anticorrosive paint vats and automated spray booths for painting. The assembly line tilted sideways for easy installation of brake, fuel, and exhaust parts. One-piece assembly of the driver instrument panel, steering column, and wheel was among the innovations at the Daewoo Motor Company not found in American plants. The plant also used robots and other automated equipment to boost quality. Finally, the car that the Daewoo Motor Company first produced—the LeMans—was based upon the Opel Kadett, which had won the 1985 "European car of the year" award. GM clearly sought not merely to follow but to accelerate, shape, and exploit the migration of knowledge about small car manufacturing to Korea. Moreover, in moving quickly to ally itself with Daewoo, GM preempted Daewoo as a partner and thereby prevented other firms from strengthening themselves by creating their own partnerships with Daewoo.

The dangers of this sort of product link spring from two sources. One is the difficulty that a firm has in helping a new organization only partly under its control to learn a wide range of skills quickly and to manufacture products for an intensely competitive market. The likelihood of frustration, or even failure, is substantial. Labor and quality problems, the appreciation of the won, and disappointing U.S. sales have strained the GM-Daewoo relationship.

In addition, if a firm succeeds in hastening the migration of knowledge to companies that will attack its adversaries, it may someday find that it, too, is under attack. IBM's PC succeeded in establishing an industry standard and thereby guided the pace and direction of knowledge in that industry segment.

Like a horseshoe magnet shaping iron filings on a piece of paper, the PC strongly influenced both hardware and software development. In the end, however, the PC also became a target of worldwide attack, which made it hard for IBM and most other companies to earn good returns in the PC business.

Neutralizing competitors. Through their alliances, GM and IBM secured supplies of the very products—small cars and small computers—that were the platforms from which its adversaries hoped to attack the more profitable large car and larger computer businesses. They, in effect, counterattacked on their adversaries' home turf using their adversaries' products.

GM's alliances gave it access to approximately 500,000 high-quality, cost-competitive small cars a year. Some had "Toyota quality" because they were manufactured with Toyota. GM's Suzuki-manufactured car achieved extraordinary gas mileage, matching at least roughly another longstanding strength of GM's Japanese competitors. In 1988, GM announced that it would combine the vehicles produced by its Japanese partners under a new nameplate, GEO. Chevrolet dealers would create separate display areas or showrooms for renamed and restyled models of the Suzuki, Isuzu, and NUMMI small cars. These, along with an imported, jeep-like sports utility vehicle made by Suzuki, would form the initial line-up of GEO vehicles. GM had created, in effect, the equivalent of a small car division, and it began advertising GEO heavily. During the first six months of 1990, GEO sales grew dramatically, and GM executives expected GEO to soon become the fourth or fifth largest selling imported nameplate in the U.S. market.

Moreover, by helping Suzuki strengthen its car business and by helping Isuzu strengthen its automobile and truck business, GM was counterattacking Toyota in its home market. Admittedly, the two small firms could do little more than nip at the heels of a giant like Toyota, but they illustrate another way in which alliances can be used to neutralize an opponent's strength. GM was also doing more than simply buttressing two small Japanese car makers that competed against Toyota. It also formed affiliations with the Nissan group, Toyota's principal competitor in Japan. Several of GM's important new parts and component relationships were with members of the Nissan group. In addition, in 1984, GM's Holden's subsidiary in Australia began supplying panels to Nissan Australia for the production of a car called the Pulsar. Nissan then supplied Pulsars to Holden's, which sold the vehicles under its own nameplate.

IBM took similar steps to neutralize its competitors in the small computer business. Its initial personal computer strategy capitalized on the migration of knowledge by creating partnerships to gain access to the knowledge. This helped IBM create its own small computer and then helped it to sell the machine. Like GM, IBM formed alliances with Japanese companies so that it, too, could counterattack its Japanese competitors in their home market with the very products, small computers, that some of them hoped to use as a launching pad from which to enter other parts of the computer business.

CONCLUSION

Like a boulder thrown into a quiet pond, the migration of knowledge has powerful, pervasive effects on companies and their industries. As competitors deploy knowledge, competition usually intensifies. Many established firms face weakening financial positions, outdated manufacturing facilities, traditional marketing assumptions and practices turned topsy-turvy, outdated company cultures, and vexing strategic dilemmas. Product links are an important way in which firms can respond to the challenge of migratory knowledge. These alliances can help them parry the threats arising from the rapid, often unpredictable movement of knowledge, enabling them to reduce costs, limit risk, accelerate speed to market, open windows on competition, build flexibility, and neutralize, at least partly, the strengths of their adversaries.

But these advantages conceal serious hazards. While product links are often a necessary part of a firm's response to the migration of knowledge, they are unlikely to be sufficient. In some ways, they are pacts with the devil. In exchange for a product today, a company helps to strengthen a competitor, providing it with distribution, technology, scale and experience economies, profits for further investment, and confidence that its products can sell successfully in its partner's markets.

More important, if a firm fills out its product line through alliances like GM's in small cars or IBM's in small computers, how much has it accomplished? Perhaps little more than to find a way of following the migration of knowledge through a succession of companies and countries. At the end of 1989, IBM was still racing neck and neck with Apple, Compaq, and its many other PC competitors. GM, through GEO, had perhaps found, after years of effort, a way to stem the erosion of its small-car market share. At best, a product link will only help a company match the products its competitors are deploying against it. Hence, the alliances discussed in this chapter are essentially defensive, and they offer little prospect of an enduring competitive advantage.

What if, for example, in the 1920s GM had attacked Ford through strategy-based product links that provided it with counterparts to Ford's enormously successful Model T? Would it have toppled Ford and become the world's car maker? Probably not. Successful strategies are built upon *unique* advantages that a firm creates for itself and then continually improves. GM defeated Ford by offering customers a wide product line of its own, through a strategy nicknamed "a car for every purse and purpose." This broad range of offerings surrounded and eventually overwhelmed the Model T. In addition, GM executives pioneered a new form of organization, the multidivision firm, which enabled the company to decentralize authority while coordinating strategic decisions through the oversight of corporate executives. These breakthroughs in strategy and organization gave GM advantages that endured for nearly half a century.[11] Similarly, when IBM introduced the System/360 in 1964, it launched itself upon a trajectory of spectacular profitability that made it the world's dominant computer company for decades. It did not seek simply to find ways of neutralizing or responding to or matching the efforts of other computer companies. It sought to leap ahead of its competitors by creating a powerful advantage that none of them possessed.[12]

In the 1980s, many firms, including GM and IBM, learned that product links alone were not an adequate solution to the problems of knowledge-driven competition. In particular, product links did not respond to the challenges and opportunities created by embedded knowledge. Hence, many firms, including GM and IBM, also relied upon a second kind of alliance, the knowledge link. Through these alliances, companies hoped to gain and create knowledge, not just to win access to products. They believed that through knowledge links they could create enduring competitive advantages. These alliances and the knowledge that has led to their creation are the subject of Chapters 4 and 5.

CHAPTER 4

Embedded Knowledge

The globalization of knowledge is not simply a matter of knowledge being created in more countries and circulated through more companies than ever before. Some knowledge is not migratory. It moves very slowly, even when its commercial value is high and firms have strong incentives to gain access to it. The reason lies, not in protectionist government policies or obstacles created by firms, but in the nature of the knowledge itself.

To understand this, one must begin with the question: where does knowledge reside? Migratory knowledge can be clearly and fully articulated—it resides in tidy, mobile packages like books and formulas, in machines, and in the minds of individuals. In contrast, embedded knowledge resides primarily in specialized relationships among individuals and groups and in the particular norms, attitudes, information flows, and ways of making decisions that shape their dealings with each other. This chapter explains embedded knowledge and shows how essential it is to the success of a firm.[1]

The boundaries of firms can either impede or hasten the slow movement of embedded knowledge. The type of alliance I have called a knowledge link, the subject of Chapter 5, is a way in which companies can learn embedded knowledge from other organizations and work with them to create it. In strategic terms, such knowledge can be crucial. Once a company has secured embedded knowledge—by dint of its own efforts, by learning from another organization, or both—it has capabilities, skills, know-how, and knowledge that are secure for a much longer period than migratory knowledge is, because embedded knowledge does not slip away so easily.

Embedded knowledge presents special challenges to firms and their managers. In the eyes of many people, the basic notion of embedded knowledge is unfamiliar and even a little threatening. In school, we learn, get grades, and advance as individuals. Much of Western political and economic theory assumes that individuals make choices on the basis of what each of them knows and values. To suppose that groups or institutions are comparable in important ways to individuals awakens fears that some large, potentially totalitarian entity can know, make decisions, and exercise rights at the expense of individual dignity and liberties. George Orwell's ever-watchful Big Brother was not an individual but a relentless collectivity.[2] The main difficulty, however, in understanding the challenge of embedded knowledge is that it requires rethinking familiar ideas about firms, their boundaries, and the work of business managers. Firms appear not as separate administrative, social, and economic spheres, but as open, porous forms of organization that learn, create, transmit, deploy, and control knowledge. They are, in essence, vast, complex repositories of embedded knowledge.

Craftsmanship

A firm embodies knowledge at many levels. The most elemental is the individual. Many people in a company have highly personal knowledge of how to accomplish particular specialized tasks. The work of Antonio Stradivari, the master violinist of the eighteenth century, vividly illustrates this sort of knowledge.[3] One authority on the violin has written that "at the age of 50 he had perfected the Stradivarius model, and no living man, although thousands of attempts have been made, has been able to produce an instrument so faultless as a Stradivarius of this period. Admirable copies have been made perfect up to the smallest detail, but the soul is always missing."[4]

Stradivari spent his life making string instruments: violas, cellos, mandolins, and guitars. But his energies were concentrated. He made no wind or percussion instruments, nor wooden clocks or furniture. Through decades of labor, Stradivari became an expert at using certain tools, woods, varnishes, and designs. His skill grew out of and depended upon a multitude of particular social relationships: Stradivari worked in a shop with his sons and others, and his predecessors and contemporaries invented and refined string instruments, while others developed and supplied the raw materials he used, evolved traditions of woodworking and instrument design, wrote music, shaped standards of taste, and bought and played his instruments. Stradivari's skills rested upon both his intimate familiarity with certain tools and materials and the particular social arrangements enveloping him.

Companies depend heavily on the same sort of highly personal knowledge. In the early years of the automobile industry, for example, workers depended upon simple, often primitive, machine tools that they controlled by hand—not the large, electrically powered, automatic, precision machines that became common after the 1920s and 1930s. They had to know how to set up their machines, maintain them, and manage their erratic operations. They needed a "feel" for their work.[5] In recent decades, many critics allege, the U.S. auto industry has been "deskilling" its workers, stripping away this knowledge and trying to transfer their skills to ever more sophisticated machines. (Roger Smith, GM's chairman in the 1980s, began his career in the auto industry with a summer job—installing glove boxes in Desotos—that required no training whatsoever.) But even at the end of the twentieth century, in an auto industry increasingly pervaded by highly technical engineering skills and computerized design techniques, much of what a chief engineer knows is not written down:

> Engineering blueprints, and symbolic design records more generally, do not contain an exhaustive account of the methods involved in the actual exercise of a productive capability. As a matter of fact, blueprints are often quite gross descriptions of

what to do, and seldom define the detailed job break-
down, much less provide "how to do it" instructions
at the job level.[6]

Similarly, an expert scheduler

> . . . is intimately familiar with products, resources,
> machines, and people who run them. Keeping in
> mind the subtleties inherent in these factors, an ex-
> pert scheduler can weave a schedule that optimizes
> yield and minimizes downtime. An expert scheduler
> is also one who knows that the "psychology of sched-
> uling" is a vital intangible. This person is a "wise old
> Turk," to use one observer's term. Here is intuition
> at work. Books, lectures, or videotapes couldn't cap-
> ture what this expert does. An extended apprentice-
> ship is necessary.[7]

Industrial research is often an individual art, not a body of technique that anybody with the right training can acquire. It depends
on individuals who have honed their talents for particular sorts
of work through years of effort. Today, despite attempts to create
automated software "factories," the actual writing of software
remains an individual craft, and the abilities of individual pro-
grammers can differ by a factor of one to twenty-five or thirty to
one.[8]
      Much of the knowledge of such craftsmen and spe-
cialists is incapable of quick migration.[9] Unlike knowledge of a
computer code or a chemical formula, it cannot be clearly and
completely communicated to someone else through words or
other symbols. Learning takes months or even years of patient,
observant apprenticeship. Moreover, a machinist, scheduler, industrial engineer, sales representative, or manager often cannot
take all his knowledge and skills to another company, because
the knowledge depends upon specific relationships: running certain types of machines, scheduling certain tasks, selling a partic-

ular product to a particular sort of customer. The eminent economist Frederick Hayek wrote in 1945:

> Today it is almost heresy to suggest that scientific knowledge is not the sum of all knowledge. But a little reflection will show that there is beyond question a body of very important but unorganized knowledge which cannot possibly be called scientific in the sense of knowledge or general rules: the knowledge of the particular circumstances of time and place. We need to remember only how much we have to learn in any occupation after we have completed our theoretical training, how big a part of our working life we spend learning particular jobs, and how valuable an asset in all walks of life is knowledge of people, of local conditions, and special circumstances. [10]

In all these cases, knowledge grows out of an intimate, working familiarity nurtured over years of effort. It resides in relationships among an individual, a particular social setting, and certain tools and tasks—not in a formula, nor in any set rules. [11] Finally, the knowledge takes the form of competence, of a capability. It is knowledge of how to do something. As we will see, a company, too, can possess exactly this kind of practical knowledge, but on a larger and more complex scale.

Teams

Just as individual craftsmen have tacit knowledge, which they cannot communicate fully to others, so do successful teams, small groups, and departments in companies. Teams bind members together in many ways, and some of them are difficult to define. [12] A recent study of effective work groups in a wide variety of organizations found that while all the groups shared certain characteristics, "each group was, in still other ways, like *no* other group, a unique entity unto itself with its own special

problems, opportunities, and ways of operating."[13] "Elusive phenomena" can matter as much to a team's performance as the
right mix of skills and expertise.[14]

       The power of subtle interactions among members of
a team and their unspoken knowledge of how they can work
together best is suggested most dramatically by cohesive athletic
teams that defeat opponents with superior individual talent, by
elite military units—the Roman Praetorian guards, the Marines,
Lawrence of Arabia's guerrillas, or Fidel Castro's insurgents—
that overcome much larger, better-equipped adversaries, and by
fledgling entrepreneurial units that wrest markets away from
larger, better-financed, and better-staffed competitors. A team's
knowledge is rooted in relationships that are even more complex
than those of craftsmen. These relationships involve a group of
individuals, the coordinated accomplishment of several tasks, and
the use of a variety of tools.[15]

       Knowledge resides in team relationships in two ways.
First, many tasks require too much knowledge for a single individual to grasp in its entirety. Hence, separate individuals, with
partial but complementary knowledge, work together as a team,
and only the team has the full body of knowledge. Consider, for
example, teams engaged in research and development. American
companies developed industrial research teams precisely because
groups of scientists and engineers could often accomplish more
than individual researchers and do so at lower cost. Groups could
share equipment, facilities, and—most important—the ideas,
techniques, perspectives, and judgments arising from a variety of
training, experience, and expertise. An historian who studied the
origins of American industrial research in the decades near the
turn of the century concluded that: "Administrators took advantage of the complementary capabilities of their researchers, sometimes setting theorists and experimentalists, abstract thinkers and
'nuts and bolts' people working together. The power of such a
team to find solutions usually surpassed the sum of the powers
of the individuals taken separately."[16] This team-based knowledge
has been dubbed "know-why": it includes knowledge about relationships, interactions, experimental results, and scientific or

engineering principles that explain why a piece of machinery or a pharmaceutical agent behaves as it does. Industrial research is often focused on complex, multitechnology, multi-expertise products and processes, and no single individual can know everything about the cause-and-effect links that determine their performance; as a whole, however, the members of a group can provide a more complete account of why a process or a product behaves as it does. [17]

The second kind of knowledge that resides in groups is more difficult to define than complementary expertise. Members of successful teams know how to work with each other. To be sure, this involves factors that can be described and managed: through statements of the group's tasks, delegation of responsibility, incentives, and so forth. [18] But other factors are more subtle and amorphous. They help create the right chemistry within a group. Something "clicks" when the right personalities, work environment, communication among team members, and leadership come together in harmony.

The paradoxical title of Tracy Kidder's *The Soul of a New Machine* points toward these elusive factors. The book describes the ambitions, pressures, personal relationships of a small team of engineers, and the frustration and elation that they experienced as they tried to create a new computer despite paltry resources and a seemingly impossible deadline. Somehow, in practice, these handicaps became spurs to success. A peculiar fusion of personalities and passions gave the team its "soul," and it created a new machine. The team got all the crucial factors exactly right. But just what were they?

Unfortunately, the full set of social arrangements that lead to outstanding R&D efforts cannot be stated in detail and then methodically put into practice by would-be innovators. They involve subtle forces of social interaction that vary from industry to industry, task to task, and group to group, and that remain frustratingly inexpressible. A recent extensive survey of the literature on organizational characteristics associated with technological innovation concluded that: "With the exception of a few internal factors that have been shown consistently to be related to innovation, studies involving the majority of the internal factors have shown confusing results."[19] Even the handful of factors that did emerge from the study—effective communication, appropriate rewards, and formalization—are general. No one has yet specified what organizational theorist William Ouchi has called "the kind of subtle reading of signals that is possible among intimate co-workers but which cannot be translated into explicit, verifiable measures."[20] Some of this knowledge is a kind of group know-how, a tacit understanding of how the people in the group can work together with the resources they have to accomplish particular tasks.

Successful teams do rely in part upon knowledge that individual members have and that they can make fully explicit. Yet their capability to perform also depends on knowledge that can be stated only partially and somewhat platitudinously by reference to mutual respect, open-mindedness, good judgment, and so forth. Much of this knowledge is not explicit; it is unwritten and sometimes even unspoken. In the words of two authorities on the transfer of technology:

> Technology might be more carefully conceptualized as a quantum of knowledge retained by individual teams of specialized personnel. This knowledge, resulting from their accumulated experience in design, production, and investment activities, is mostly tacit. . . . It is acquired in problem-solving and trouble-shooting activities within the firm, remaining there in a substantially unmodified state.[21]

One learns how to be a member of a team either by joining it or through an apprenticeship of some sort. Marines learn to work and fight as Marines in bootcamp and in combat, not through mail-order instruction manuals. Much of the crucial knowledge that resides in teams can be glimpsed only by their members, and often none of them knows all that the team knows.

Firms

A firm is an embodiment of knowledge: it can learn, remember, and know things that none of the individuals or teams within it know. It is, in essence, a very large team, or a confederation of teams, in which enormously complex skills and knowledge are embedded in the minds of its members and in the formal and informal social relationships that orchestrate their efforts.[22]

Consider the example of the Toyota production system, the entire constellation of operating policies, traditions, norms, and routine practices that the Toyota Motor Company has evolved over the past fifty years. It includes the just-in-time (kanban) inventory system, participative labor management relations, and intense commitment to the success of the Toyota "family" of affiliated companies. By perfecting the "Toyota way," the company has become one of the most profitable and powerful companies in the world.

Toyota's knowledge of how to make cars lies embedded in highly specialized social and organizational relationships that have evolved through decades of common effort. It rests in routines, information flows, ways of making decisions, shared attitudes and expectations, and specialized knowledge that Toyota managers, workers, suppliers and purchasing agents, and others have about different aspects of their business, about each other, and about how they all can work together. None of these parties knows what Toyota as a whole "knows" about making cars.

How does a firm learn what it knows? Its knowledge is drawn from myriad sources. Some of it, the smaller fraction, comes from explicit efforts such as market research, R&D, or licensing technology from other firms. Much else is learned by doing: through the countless, small, daily endeavors in which sales representatives learn about customers, supervisors learn about workers and machinery, and purchasing agents learn about suppliers, and through endless adjustments to the routines by which all of them coordinate behavior and judgments with each other. The experience curve—the tendency for the cost of making

or doing something to fall as a firm gains more experience—
reflects the fact that knowledge born of specialized experience
becomes embedded in a company's routines. Hiroyuki Itami, a
Japanese business scholar, argues that the most valuable assets of
firms are invisible—they are information-based assets such as
consumer trust, brand image, corporate culture, and management skill—and that they are learned by the whole organization.
He writes that "the firm's invisible assets are no more or less than
the accumulated efforts of everyone in the organization."[23]

How does a firm remember what it knows? In part,
through a "memory" that consists of its standard operating procedures, the formal and informal routines its members use to get
their work accomplished.[24] Organizational theorists began un-
earthing the crucial role of organizational routines in the late
1950s and early 1960s. More recently, two economists, Richard
Nelson and Sidney Winter, have deepened this perspective, ar-
guing that "organizations remember by doing."[25] Some of what
an organization remembers and knows is, of course, stored in
the memories of individual members of the organization; some
is stored on paper and in computers. But all these individual, localized bodies of knowledge form a large and complex
whole:

> Without the crane operator's ability to
> interpret the hand signal for "down a little more"
> and to lower the hook accordingly, the abilities to
> perceive the need for the signal and to generate it are
> meaningless. To view organizational memory as re-
> ducible to individual memories is to overlook, or un-
> dervalue, the linking of these individual memories by
> shared experiences in the past, experiences that have
> established the extremely detailed and specified com-
> munication system that underlies routine
> performance.[26]

In what sense does a firm "think"? The answer is
implicit in Chester Barnard's widely quoted statement that "the

first executive function is to develop and maintain a system of communication." For Barnard, the business executive who wrote a seminal work in organization theory, the communication system transmits not only hard data but also "intangible facts, opinions, suggestions, and suspicions" through what he calls the "compatibility of personnel."[27] Organizations "think" and "decide" by processing—transmitting, altering, refining, elaborating, ignoring, and combining—both hard and soft information.

Herbert A. Simon first conceptualized the firm as an information-processing system. In his path-breaking book, *Administrative Behavior*, Simon writes:

> The anatomy of an organization viewed as a decision-making and information-processing system may look very different from the anatomy of the same organization viewed as a collection of people. The latter viewpoint, which is a traditional one, focuses attention on the groupings of human beings— that is, the departmentalization. The former viewpoint, on the other hand, focuses on the decision-making process itself—that is, upon the flows and transformations of symbols.[28]

More recently, economist Kenneth Arrow has described the firm as an "incompletely connected network of information flows."[29] Economist Oliver Williamson has conceptualized firms as institutional devices for efficiently overcoming problems arising from the limits on individual knowledge and rationality.[30]

Some of the relationships through which firms process information are formal and explicit, such as the arrangements through which the head of an overseas subsidiary reports to a vice president for international operations; some are tangible, even physical, such as the links in a firm's telephone and computer network. But companies also depend on informal relationships shaped by elusive phenomena such as attitudes, common expectations, camaraderie, trust, loyalty, and unwritten norms and shared values. In the past decade, business academics and the business press have referred to these as a company's "culture." The sociologist Philip Selznick, writing in the 1950s, coined the term "distinctive competence" to indicate the role these factors play in an organization's success or failure. A firm's distinctive competence is its capability to perform particular tasks more effectively than comparable organizations. It rests not only on hard economic assets like capital, equipment, and machinery, but also on the particular character of an organization as a human community.[31]

Logicians warn of the fallacy of misplaced concreteness, and the bald statement that firms know and think in the same ways as individuals would be an instance of this error. But Polanyi, Nelson, Winter, Simon, Arrow, Williamson, and Selznick stress a different point: that organizations, through formal and informal relationships, do create, store, and process information. Organizations do not know what they know in the same way as individuals, but knowledge and capabilities do reside in the interstices of their routines, practices, cultures, and working relationships.

Outside Organizations

Many important relationships in which knowledge and capabilities are embedded are not inside the firm. Close relationships between a firm and an external organization often provide the chance for specialized knowledge and capabilities to take root and grow. A good instance of such growth is the relationship between many large Japanese manufacturing companies and their suppliers.

The Toyota Motor Company, for example, is not simply a single independent company. It is a confederation, more properly called the Toyota Group. Like Nissan, Hitachi, and many other large Japanese manufacturers, Toyota is at the core of a vast network of firms consisting of hundreds of primary, secondary, and tertiary suppliers. The dominant firm in these networks concentrates on assembly work and marketing. Primary suppliers constitute the next tier. In Toyota's case, they make engine and brake parts, meters, chassis, and bodies. Beneath them is a tier of secondary subcontractors that supplies the primary suppliers. They, in turn, rely upon hundreds of tertiary suppliers, most of which are small and produce the simple "parts of parts" that secondary contractors use to make their own products.

Even though each firm remains legally separate, the members of these groups are connected to each other through a multitude of intricate relationships. Among them are minority equity ownership (Toyota owns 10–70% of the shares of many of its affiliated firms), interlocking boards of directors, and financial aid in the form of trade credits, loans, or credit guarantees given by the parent company. The presidents of the affiliated companies meet regularly, and the peak firm sometimes lends personnel and offers technological guidance and exchange to other group members. Firms at each tier of the hierarchy purchase a high fraction of their suppliers' outputs. The relationship among group members is best described as semi-permanent, for although it is unusual for one of these relationships to be terminated or for one supplier in a group to replace another, it does happen occasionally.

Many of these group relationships originated in the 1950s, when automotive firms and other manufacturers lacked the funds to invest in component operations. Wages and benefits were also lower among subcontractors, and few of their employees were assured lifetime jobs. Other group relationships had formed decades or even centuries earlier. Nevertheless, in the 1950s and 1960s, as Japanese manufacturers grew larger and more prosperous, these relationships did not wither away, but were refined and restructured. The reason that the relationships endured lies, in large measure, in the knowledge embedded in them. Through decades of experience together, the Toyota Group firms and their managers and employees have learned each other's particular capabilities, technologies, routines, and needs.[32]

Consider, for example, the so-called Toyota production system and, in particular, its reliance on kanban, or just-in-time, operations.[33] JIT refers to the notion that a component should arrive where it is needed precisely when it is needed. A kanban itself is simply a small paper or metal tag attached to a container of automobile parts or components, describing its destination, indicating when it should arrive, and so forth. But the kanban system is more than a scheduling device. Toyota executives call the kanban system "the essence of Toyota and its relationships."

The system requires intimate, continuous, and detailed working relationships and information flows among firms.[34] When it succeeds, the approach reveals bottlenecks, lessens the need for managers and supervisors, and permits a plant to ship products more quickly. Toyota executives also believe it gives members of the group a common interest in finding and anticipating problems, thereby allowing them to focus on their joint concern: manufacturing outstanding products. It is not, they stress, merely a system for highlighting problems or for figuring out who is to blame for them.[35]

Koichi Shimokawa, a professor of business administration at Hosei University in Tokyo, attributes the success of these relationships to several factors, among them "informality" and "emotional trust."[36] Taiichi Ohno, the original developer of the kanban system, said that the company "can approach the perfect realization of this system . . . only if Toyota shares its destiny with the surrounding cooperative manufacturers as a single community."[37] Toyota's supplier relations depend on complex expectations, norms, and routines. These are social as well as technical, tacit as well as explicit, and they also create, store, and process information. In the words of one Japanese economist, the relationships are "vertical information structures."[38]

Group Affiliations

Knowledge can also be embedded in looser affiliations between a company and other organizations. Business groups are one example. In recent years, large Japanese enterprise groups such as Mitsubishi, Hitachi, Mitsui, Nissan, and Toyota have gained prominence because of Japan's economic success and because U.S. and Japanese firms, including GM and IBM, have formed relationships with firms that belong to these groups. Two economists have described Japanese firms as enmeshed in a "thick and complex skein of relations matched in no other country."[39]

Toyota, Hitachi, and Nissan represent one kind of Japanese business group: federations of supplier firms centered on a single, dominant manufacturing company.[40] The other kind, represented by Mitsui, Mitsubishi, and Sumitomo, are contemporary descendants of the zaibatsu, the giant conglomerates that dominated Japanese industrial life for most of the first half of this century. Their member firms included banks, insurance companies, light and heavy industrial firms, and overseas trading companies. The U.S. occupation broke up the zaibatsu in an attempt to disperse their economic and political power: later many of the original groups reemerged, though with much looser and more informal ties among the members. Presidents of member companies meet regularly, often monthly, and their executives serve on the boards of directors of other group firms. Members generally own a small fraction of each other's shares and rely more heavily for funds on banks and other financial institutions in their group. They also buy and sell goods from each other more frequently than from outside firms. Social ties among member firms often have deep roots; the Mitsui Group, for example, can trace its origins to the early seventeenth century.[41]

Members of the Japanese enterprise groups that descended from the zaibatsu—such as Mitsui and Mitsubishi—are connected to each other by much looser ties than the firms in the Toyota or Hitachi supplier hierarchies. Their relationships serve many purposes, including the creation, communication, and refinement of knowledge.[42] For example, many of the large enterprise groups that descend from the zaibatsu include trading companies, or *sogo shosha*, as they are called in Japan. A recent study describes them this way:

Like Adam Smith's "Invisible Hand" of
the market and like Alfred Chandler's "Visible Hand"

of the vertically integrated firm, the sogo shosha provide a system of governance, channeling money, information, ideas, raw materials, products, services,
and other economic goods into a coherent system of
activity. The nature of this role is elusive, for it cuts
across established categories of economic institutional
analysis.[43]

The authors conclude that networks of personal relationships
linking employees of the trading company to one another and to
the firms they serve are "the single most important aspect of the
management systems of the sogo shosha. . . . they account for
much of the institution's capacity to cope with diversity, complexity, and change." The authors found that these networks
depend on four characteristics—commitment, understanding,
credibility, and obligation.[44] The networks provide the capability
of gathering, coordinating, assessing, and communicating knowledge on a vast scale.[45]

　　　Within enterprise groups, the meetings of "presidents' clubs" also serve as forums for exchanging information and
coordinating interfirm activities. A Japanese scholar gave this
overview:

　　　It is difficult to know from the outside
what is being discussed and what kind of information
is exchanged at the meetings. Judging from fragmen-
tary evidence obtained from interviews and newspa-
pers, the main topics of these meetings include the
opening up of business opportunities, new technologies, government regulations, foreign market situations, the granting of permission to a firm to use the
group name, and the assignment of contributions to
be made to charitable organizations from among
member firms.[46]

He describes Japanese enterprise groups as "information clubs"—
social devices for sharing information on technological devel-

opments and investment opportunities, which work more efficiently and with less risk than market mechanisms. For example, in handling migratory knowledge, the group relationships reduce the chance that potentially valuable information will escape and be deployed against its members by firms outside the group. Long-term relationships based on trust and a sense of common enterprise also reduce the risk that one member will ruthlessly exploit information taken from another member.

Geography and Knowledge

Knowledge and capabilities can also reside in geographic regions—in the interstices of the social, financial, technological, and managerial relationships that can link nearby organizations. Lester Hogan, the former president of Fairchild Semiconductor, made this observation about Silicon Valley in California:

> There's a magic here in Silicon Valley
> that we don't understand. This critical mass took
> some years to build up; it had its roots in the 1950s,
> but it really began to blossom in the 1980s. And Silicon Valley has been a really special kind of information environment ever since. An intellectual pot is
> boiling here.[47]

An experienced semiconductor engineer from Silicon Valley said, "I know someone, and they know someone. But I don't know who they know. The power of this network is that the participants all know that it exists. We all know that we all know lots of other people in the Valley."[48] To find business opportunities in these networks, a consortium of Japanese firms based in Osaka created a consulting firm, Osaka-California Linkage Technology Center, with headquarters in San Jose, California.

In the late 1980s, the Greater Tokyo area continued to draw people from the rest of Japan, despite its stratospheric housing costs, overcrowding, noise, and pollution. Among the

96   THE KNOWLEDGE LINK

reasons was Tokyo's role as a vast information network. By moving there, individuals and companies can link themselves more
easily with the government, financial markets, other Japanese
companies, and foreign firms. (One Japanese executive, asked
why the migration to Tokyo persisted despite so many incon-
veniences, answered that people move there because it is the
center. Asked why it was the center, he responded: because so
many people move there.) Wall Street, the City of London, and
Route 128 near Boston are all examples of large, loose, social
complexes in which knowledge and know-how are embedded.
Manchester during the Industrial Revolution, Florence in the
Renaissance, and Vienna at the turn of the century all fall within
the genus of large, loose, intellectually or economically fecund
communities.[49]

In his study of successful industries in ten countries,
Michael Porter notes the propinquity of many of these nations'
successful industries. Examples include German industries in
metalworking, industries in Israel related to agriculture, and
Swedish industries in pulp and paper. Porter writes that "information flows freely and innovations diffuse rapidly through the
conduits of customers and suppliers who have contact with multiple competitors. Interconnections within the cluster, often un-
anticipated, lead to the perception of new ways of competing and
entirely new opportunities. People and ideas combine in new
ways."[50]

THE CHALLENGES OF EMBEDDED KNOWLEDGE

Embedded knowledge in its many forms poses a fundamentally different challenge for companies than migratory
knowledge. The migration of knowledge intensifies battles over
products. One company invents and sells a product; another
copies it, sometimes improves it, and then makes and sells it at
a lower price. In extreme cases, as in the commodity personal-
computer business, knowledge migrates around the world in

search of low-cost production sites, and a cut-throat global battle ensues.

Embedded knowledge leads to battles fought with capabilities as well as products. More and more companies around the world are developing specialized capabilities that enable them to manufacture cheaply, design innovatively, bring products to market quickly, or perceive and respond to customer needs more precisely. Today's product battle may be only one episode in a longer war, in which the victor will be the company with the strongest capability to invent, make, and sell a *stream* of future products. Of course, embedded knowledge does not always represent a challenge to other firms. The Soviet economy, for example, has been a vast system of embedded knowledge in which the capability of performing economic activities slowly, poorly, expensively, and grudgingly is deeply ingrained in social, political, and economic relationships.

The challenge for a company arises when it is confronted by competitors capable of working faster, more flexibly, more efficiently, more cost-effectively, or more imaginatively than itself; or when it seeks to enhance its own capabilities or create new ones; or when it needs to gain access to knowledge and skills that are embedded in relationships outside its boundaries. In each of these situations, embedded knowledge, which by its very nature is inaccessible, presents a different challenge than migratory knowledge. Reading a book about another company's operations or hiring away one of its managers will not enable a firm to secure the knowledge it seeks.

The challenge becomes especially daunting in a world in which many companies have highly specialized, sometimes unique capabilities. Clearly, the firm with the capability to work faster, better, or cheaper than its competitors has a powerful advantage, one that cannot migrate away quickly. A firm that needs to create these capabilities or gain access to them faces a difficult challenge, and the three classic approaches to strengthening a firm's capabilities may prove inadequate. These approaches include: using arm's-length market transactions to buy resources from other organizations, "going-it-alone," and relying on mergers and acquisitions.

Market Transactions

Managers secure many important resources from other organizations through arm's-length, competitive transactions in the marketplace. Markets communicate some forms of knowledge quite well. The price mechanism is a brilliant communication device for certain purposes. In competitive markets, prices are a simple, readily understood method for distilling and communicating a wide range of judgments about scarcity, need, and value, now and in the future. Such information plays a vital role in allocating society's resources. Rising prices indicate opportunities and attract resources; declining prices discourage investment.

The price mechanism works less effectively, however, for transactions involving information and knowledge. Consider a situation in which one party wants to sell a simple piece of knowledge to another. The seller confronts what economists call the "paradox of information." For the buyer and seller to agree on the price of information, the buyer must assess its value. However, in the words of economist Kenneth Arrow, "Its value for the purchaser is not known until he has the information, but then he has in effect acquired it without cost."[51] This problem is especially acute for transactions involving migratory knowledge, which is available in dangerously mobile packages.

When knowledge is embedded, particular problems arise.[52] This knowledge is not available in simple, unitized packages that can be bought for cash. For one organization to secure embedded knowledge from another, its personnel must have direct, intimate, and extensive exposure to the social relationships of the other organization. The company needs to find ways to permit staff, equipment, ideas, and sometimes even cultural traits to flow across its boundaries.

In such situations, arm's-length market dealings do

not work well. Consider, for example, two different relationships between a firm and a supplier.[53] In one, a company is buying an industrial commodity. If many suppliers can provide the product, then the buyer can simply write a short-term contract with the supplier that offers the best terms. The market relationship handles uncertainty: if the buyer needs more or less of the raw material, it can write a new contract with another supplier or change the terms of the original contract when it comes up for renewal. If the supplier is greedy and tries to exploit its relationship with the buyer—perhaps by threatening to withhold a shipment at the last minute—the buyer can take legal action and, later, punish the supplier by refusing to renew the contract.

      In contrast, consider what happens if the company and its supplier try to use arm's-length market arrangements to learn capabilities from each other and combine them in a unique way. If the parties need to collaborate over a long period of time in order to create and commercialize something new, it makes little sense to have a short-term contract, giving each the option of terminating the relationship at an early date. But a long-term contract will be difficult to write. At the beginning of the project, both parties may have a fairly clear idea about what they *hope* will happen, but they know much less about what actually *will* happen once the collaboration begins. They have no experience working with each other and they want to jointly produce something novel. Several possible scenarios open up.

      They could, for example, try to write a long contract detailing the contingencies they foresee and the precise responsibilities of each party under each contingency. Unfortunately, such a contract is costly—an attorney's paradise. Moreover, companies planning to do customized work involving state-of-the-art technologies can hardly specify which party has what rights to the particular forms of intellectual and physical property the joint endeavor is likely to create. Because of uncertainty and the limits of human foresight, the contract would probably omit important contingencies. When unanticipated circumstances arose, each party could try to take advantage of the other. And, even if one party clearly violated the contract, it could be costly, time-consuming, and self-defeating for the other to seek to enforce its rights.

GM has tried to create a North American hybrid of the Toyota production system through a long, complex, and, at times, frustrating effort. Scores of GM managers and thousands of workers have worked at NUMMI or at least visited the operation. It would have been much simpler for GM to buy from Toyota the manual *How to Create the Toyota Production System*, but the document does not exist and, in a fundamental sense, could not be written. Much of what Toyota "knows" resides in routines, company culture, and long-established working relationships in the Toyota Group.

In essence, the capability-sharing, capability-creating relationship between the companies requires something other than a traditional market transaction. The two parties become dependent on each other, sometimes heavily so. Both have a stake in the asset, the joint capability, that they are creating. This makes them reluctant to walk away, and thus each can be exploited by the other. Both are subject to the vagaries of an uncertain future whose risks cannot be fully covered in a detailed contract. Once the two parties have gone even a short way down the path toward collaboration, arm's-length market relationships fail to meet the intrinsic requirements of the tasks that the company and its supplier face.

Going-It-Alone

To avoid the problems of market contracting, a company could opt to develop capabilities on its own. The basic problem with the "go-it-alone" approach is that autonomous efforts are often slow and limiting: they are dangerous in a world of specialized capabilities, shortening product life cycles, and time-based competition, where windows for earning profits open and slam shut quickly. Companies do need to pursue go-it-alone strategies for crucial resources, core capabilities, and key technologies. But the worldwide creation of embedded knowledge makes it increasingly hard for them to use this strategy for all the supporting capabilities a company may need.

The difficulties of a go-it-alone strategy are evident when we consider what the purchase of a car might be like 15 or 20 years from now. Customers will shop at home by computer, but not on today's terminals connected to a tangle of wires, TV-like boxes, telephones, and other gear. Instead, shoppers will use wall-sized, high-resolution, three-dimensional screens that respond to voice commands and questions. The screens will display a multitude of cars and let customers, in effect, walk around the cars, choose and display different options, and even simulate driving. The home computer—actually, a supercomputer—will also provide information on the performance of cars and financing options.

Buyers will be able to test-drive cars either by requesting a dealer to bring a car to their home or by going to a shopping mall "micro-dealer," an operation consisting of a simulator and a few vehicles available for test-driving. After making a choice, customers will place their orders through a telecommunications and computer network that connects the dealer—or their living room—with a "factory of the future," which will use computer-controlled technology to produce customized vehicles, perhaps within a week or two of the order. The factory itself will be connected to its suppliers and subsuppliers through yet another telecommunications network.

The car of the future will contain far more electronics than today's vehicles. In fact, by the late 1990s, electronics are likely to account for almost a third of a car's total cost. Automobiles will soon contain several computers, each with the power of today's most sophisticated personal computers (which now handle as many as six million operations per second). Computers will manage traction to prevent tires from spinning on slippery roads; "active" suspension systems that spot bumps and potholes and adjust each wheel for them; avoidance radar to alert drivers to possible collisions; and image enhancement devices to help drivers see through fog. Other computerization will include engine-control microprocessors, antitheft devices that actually

prevent thefts, advanced on-board diagnostic tools, and naviga-
tion systems that use video screens to display a car's location and
show the quickest route to a destination. Electronic sensors in
cars and along roads might even guide or control vehicles. Researchers at Volkswagen and other companies believe that such
systems would increase safety, reduce polluting emissions, and
enable more cars to use roadways by packing them together
closely, even at high speeds. [54]

Of course, such futuristic sketches are speculative.
They extrapolate current trends and assume that advanced electronics can be introduced at reasonable costs, that customers will
pay for these innovations, and that mechanics and road crews
could maintain cars and streets that are actually computers on
wheels or in concrete. What these sketches make clear, however,
are the increasing difficulties that auto firms and computer firms
will face in pursuing go-it-alone strategies.

The scenario suggests that automobile firms will need
a wide range of capabilities that lie outside the industry as pres-
ently defined. These include in-depth capabilities in computer
science, information systems, aerospace, materials science, and
robotics. In short, the traditional boundaries separating a number
of industries will collapse. The automobile industry, once considered mature, will rapidly demature and will enter a long period of turbulence and ferment. As this happens, the companies
that supply the auto industry, such as the computer industry,
will evolve quickly and will need to draw upon nontraditional
capabilities.

The destruction of traditional boundaries separating
industries is only one of the factors that will make it necessary
for firms to have a growing range of capabilities. The other is
the continued proliferation of capabilities within industries. Consider, for example, how the past ten or fifteen years of the computer industry have looked from the perspective of IBM. In the
mid-1970s, IBM was still benefiting from the spectacularly successful go-it-alone strategy through which it created the 360 series
in the early 1960s. The 360 made IBM the world's dominant

computer firm and reduced its competitors to the status of also-, rans, referred to disdainfully as "the dwarfs" or "the bunch."[55] In the early 1970s, IBM forged further ahead with its 370 series, incorporating the then-new technology of integrated circuits.

By the mid-1980s, new technologies and capabilities were burgeoning outside IBM's central sphere of expertise, the production and sale of mainframe computers. Dozens of firms around the world were racing to produce faster and faster micro-processors, which would soon make it possible to have "main-frames on a chip." As computer power grew cheaper and more widely available, more companies began developing specialized software and peripheral equipment to meet the rapidly multiply-ing uses of computers. Thousands of small companies concen-trated on particular segments of the computer business, such as storage devices, controllers and fiber optic devices to manage networks, message-switching systems, and modems.

Other companies such as Digital Equipment Cor-poration and AT&T were developing technology and software enabling them to link hundreds of computers into a single net-work. Customers were responding to the proliferation of tech-nologies and capabilities by demanding that computer vendors sell them, not individual chunks of hardware, but integrated systems of hardware and software customized to their distinctive data-processing and business needs. EDS, for example, was build-ing a global data-processing, telecommunications, and factory automation network for GM. This would ultimately link the hundreds of IBM mainframes and hundreds of thousands of com-puter terminals throughout GM. As customers demanded larger, more complex networks, opportunities arose for small niche firms to provide specialized hardware and software for these customers. Also, the customers themselves often developed their own spe-cialized software for their networks. When a multitude of spe-cialized capabilities bursts forth in an industry, as in the case of computers, or when they dissolve the barriers among industries, as in the case of automobiles, go-it-alone strategies are increas-ingly problematic.

Mergers and Acquisitions

A company that needs to gain new capabilities often tries to avoid both of the problems we have just discussed—the limits of market transactions and the difficulties of a go-it-alone strategy—by acquiring or merging with a firm that has the knowledge or capabilities that it needs. But this approach has serious handicaps. Sometimes there are practical problems—GM, for example, did not have the option of acquiring Fanuc, the robotics company. A jewel of Japan's high-tech economy, it was simply not for sale. The same holds true for the capabilities of university laboratories.

However, when this barrier recedes, a second appears: at some point, limited financial and managerial resources bring a company's efforts at vertical integration to a halt. Even the largest and wealthiest companies such as IBM and GM do not have the resources to acquire all of the thousands of suppliers and dealers on which they depend. A rich firm can, of course, acquire the most crucial capabilities—if it can afford the acquisition cost and if there are no legal barriers—but it will not be able to buy every company that has knowledge likely to prove useful to it in the future.

But even when acquisitions are possible, another hazard emerges. Mergers and acquisitions often threaten to impair or even destroy the operating practices and the sense of trust, independence, and entrepreneurship on which a firm's special capabilities rest. Mergers threaten, in the words of one GM executive, to "rationalize away partners' business knowledge." Such concerns are the reasons why so many announcements of mergers and acquisitions include a pledge that the acquired firm will be free to operate autonomously. Too often, in pursuit of synergy or cost control, a merged company finds that its managers have lost their authority, its operating units have been broken up and merged with those of the acquiring company, its fighting spirit and distinctive culture have been diluted or lost, and its most talented personnel have moved on. To the extent that a company's knowledge and capabilities depend on its culture and spirit, a merger threatens to destroy the very thing that it was intended to secure. Finally, even if a magic wand could dispel these problems, an acquisition makes little sense when a company is interested in learning only one of the many capabilities of another organization or when markets or technology may change quickly. Tomorrow's needs may differ from today's, and an acquisition may become an albatross around a company's neck.

Under these circumstances, the most successful response to the need for new capabilities is a particular kind of strategic alliance, a knowledge link. Less permanent than an acquisition or merger, it is at the same time more targeted and efficient. It allows companies to gain knowledge they need without disturbing the delicate balance of social relationships in which the knowledge is contained.

CHAPTER 5

Knowledge Links

Managers are playing with fire when their company does not own and control its crucial resources, core capabilities, and key technologies. But what about the knowledge, resources, and skills that play supporting roles? As embedded knowledge and specialized capabilities are created in a growing number of companies and other organizations around the world, firms often find it too costly and cumbersome to develop, on their own, all the knowledge and capabilities they need or want to have available. In the words of IBM president, Jack Kuehler, "It's a dangerous thing to think we know everything."[1]

In response, many firms are creating knowledge links—alliances that give them access to the skills and capabilities of other organizations and sometimes enable them to work with other organizations to create new capabilities. Knowledge links can be tactical or strategic. A single knowledge link can help a company build new skills in a limited area of its operations. This is a tactical effort. In contrast, when a company creates a multitude of knowledge links with customers, suppliers, labor organizations, universities, and other organizations, and when these alliances strengthen each other and support the company's long-term objectives, then knowledge links are genuinely strategic.

This is how GM and IBM have sought to use many of their knowledge links during the 1980s. Their new knowledge-intensive relationships have played important supporting roles in each company's effort to renew and reshape its core capabilities and to change the competitive rules of the game in its favor. Such major strategic efforts are usually accompanied by changes in organizational structure, and this has been the case at both IBM and GM. They are now structured more like city-states and less like citadels, because of their growing reliance on knowledge-rich alliances. Like city-states, each firm has at its core a dense network of relationships defined by ownership, control, and social bonds. It is no longer easy to define what is inside and outside the two companies. Instead, each firm is linked to other organizations through a multitude of arrangements in which control and ownership are shared, social bonds blurred, classical contracting compromised, and embedded knowledge is transferred, renewed, and created.

GM and IBM, like many other American firms, would be creating far fewer knowledge links today if it were not for the economic threats posed by competitors in Japan and elsewhere. By the 1980s, many of these foreign competitors had combined knowledge they had secured from the United States with their indigenous capabilities and were vying for the lead in worldwide technology and product contests. Sometimes, they held the lead. In the mid-1980s, for example, Toyota and other Japanese auto companies were pioneers in introducing powerful multivalve engines. At the same time, Japanese and U.S. car makers were racing each other to develop small, fuel-efficient, low-cost two-stroke engines and "active suspension systems" that electronically sensed road conditions and adjusted a car's ride. In computers, Fujitsu sold mainframes that ran faster than comparably priced IBM machines. (In the 1970s, a single American firm, Cray Research, had dominated the supercomputer field.) By the late 1980s, breakthroughs were taking place at Fujitsu, Hitachi, and NEC, as well as at small, startup firms in the United States such as Sequent and Thinking Machines. These products were the progeny of highly refined and specialized capabilities. Companies and countries were competing to develop, not just the latest products, but the capabilities to develop, refine, and sometimes revolutionize these products year after year.

American firms often create product links in response to such developments, thereby quickly securing products that other companies already have. Knowledge links do more. They are, in effect, a higher step in an evolutionary chain of alliances. Like product links, their forebears, they usually produce products or services, and they can also help to reduce risks, cut costs, increase speed to market, and so forth. But knowledge links also help the partners learn and sometimes create new capabilities. In fact, this is often a prerequisite for the alliance's success: without acquiring new knowledge, many partnerships could not produce the products or services that its parent organizations want.

CHARACTERISTICS OF KNOWLEDGE LINKS

The first distinguishing trait of knowledge links is that learning and creating knowledge is a central objective of the alliance. Knowledge links can help one company learn specialized capabilities from another; they can help a company combine its special capabilities with those of another organization to create new embedded knowledge; and they can enable one company to help another organization build up its skills and capabilities in ways that will benefit both companies later on.

Second, knowledge links are more intimate than product links. In order for two organizations to learn, create, or strengthen specialized capabilities, personnel from each must work together closely. This would not be the case if the companies were trying to transfer migratory knowledge: then they could simply exchange cash for a book of blueprints or a set of formulas. When companies seek to learn embedded knowledge from each other, their relationship resembles that of a master and an apprentice, which Michael Polanyi describes in this way:

> You follow your master because you trust his manner of doing things even when you cannot analyze and account in detail for its effectiveness. By watching the master and emulating his efforts in the presence of his example, the apprentice learns unconsciously, picks up the rules of the art, including those which are not explicitly known to the master

himself. These hidden rules can be assimilated only by a person who surrenders himself uncritically to the imitation of another.[2]

The third distinctive feature of knowledge links is the extraordinarily wide range of partners with which these links can be formed. Product links are usually formed with competitors or potential competitors. GM, as we have seen, turned to four Asian car companies to help it fill the small car gap in its product line. Knowledge links, in contrast, can be formed with virtually any other organization—as long as it has a specialized capability to contribute to the partnership. Through knowledge links, buyers and suppliers can share expertise on manufacturing processes and work together to improve both the buyer's product and the components the supplier provides. Through knowledge links, university laboratories and companies share and create knowledge. Knowledge links can also include participatory, cooperative relations between companies and their workers and labor unions. Through these, managers learn from workers how to make higher-quality products and how to do so more cheaply and efficiently. At the same time, company-union alliances often involve extensive training programs, so that workers become "multiskilled": instead of performing simple, repetitive tasks, workers develop, as individuals and as teams, the broader range of capabilities that a company needs.

Finally, knowledge links differ from product links because of their greater strategic potential. Product links help one company catch up, buy time, defend itself, or recapture its investment in fixed costs by selling the product quickly and in high volume through partners around the world. Knowledge links can help a firm extend or modify one of its basic capabilities, and a constellation of knowledge links can contribute to a larger strategic effort to renew core capabilities or create new ones.

Knowledge links and product links differ more sharply in theory than in practice. Both are members of the same organizational species, corporate alliances, and both blur traditional firm boundaries through shared ownership and control, linked social systems, and departures from classical, arm's-length contracting. The two kinds of alliances often differ from each other in degree, not in kind. Just as the evolution of life has proceeded through trial-and-error adaptation to varied circumstances, so alliances have produced a spectrum of hybrids in response to the needs of companies. At one end are nearly pure cases of product links, where learning is much less important than access to a product or wider distribution for an existing product. At the other end, the parties seek to learn or create new capabilities as well as to develop a new product. Many alliances fall into the middle ranges of this spectrum.

The GM-Suzuki alliance and IBM's early PC alliances fall nearer the end of the spectrum defined by pure product links. In these alliances, learning played a small role. Neither company sought to learn new capabilities or to achieve a product breakthrough. To be sure, the parties did need to learn enough about each other to coordinate activities, and Suzuki needed to learn from GM about its product specifications and U.S. regulations. Suzuki also received some engineering assistance from GM. But the main aim of the alliance was not for GM to learn from Suzuki, nor for Suzuki to learn from GM. GM needed a product quickly, and Suzuki wanted financing for a subcompact it had designed and access to distribution in the United States without the cost and risk of creating its own dealer network. This alliance, in its early phases, was a nearly pure case of a product link.

The GM-Daewoo alliance involved more learning than the GM-Suzuki deal, but mainly for Daewoo, which learned about many aspects of automobile manufacture. While GM learned more about the Korean market, its principal aim was to secure another source of low-cost small cars, and it was not creating a new product. GM provided Daewoo with existing GM technology and a vehicle from its Adam Opel subsidiary that GM was already making and selling in West Germany. In doing so, GM did not develop new knowledge or capabilities. The Daewoo alliance, for GM, was a product link; for Daewoo, a knowledge link.

NUMMI was a more complex hybrid. It was, in part, a product link, providing GM with access to a large number of very high-quality small cars. The product was not new (it was a car Toyota was already making and selling in Japan), but NUMMI helped both companies learn and create new capabilities. It helped Toyota learn about managing U.S. workers, suppliers, and trucking firms, and about dealing with the UAW and state and local governments. GM gained the opportunity to learn firsthand about the Toyota production system—its collaborative approach to worker and supplier relations, its just-in-time inventory management, and its highly efficient plant management. Most important, both companies were jointly creating new knowledge and capabilities, each experimenting with a United States-Japanese way of managing an auto plant.

Further along the spectrum was the alliance announced in early 1990 by IBM and Siemens, the West German electronics giant. In this case, the partners planned to pool existing skills and to acquire new ones in the design, manufacture, and testing of computer chips, in order to develop chips two generations more sophisticated than any on the market. To be sure, IBM brought greater technological prowess to the alliance, and, like a product link, the partnership would manufacture a product and reduce the partners' financial risks (designing an advanced microchip and building a plant were expected to cost over $1 billion). But the creation of new capabilities played a vital role in the partnership and in this way it differed dramatically from the GM-Suzuki or IBM PC alliances.

EXTENDING CAPABILITIES THROUGH ALLIANCES

When go-it-alone strategies, classic market transactions, or mergers and acquisitions seem unable to meet a company's needs, knowledge links can help a company gain access to the capabilities of other organizations or work with them to create new capabilities. One of GM's knowledge links, the GMFanuc Robotics Corporation (GMF), demonstrates how a knowledge link can help two companies turn the challenges of embedded knowledge into opportunities for each firm to extend and broaden its capabilities.[3]

In 1982, GM and Fanuc, the Japanese controls and robotics company, each invested $5 million to create GMF. Its charter was to design, market, service, and develop applications for factory automation robots. Technology would flow to and from GMF's parents, without royalties or licenses. GMF expected to move far beyond "duck-drinking-water" robots that perform the same simple task at the same spot on the same product time and time again. Future robots would have sensory functions; they would use television cameras and laser beams or extend sensitive probes to locate objects, reducing the need for manufacturers to develop ways of aligning objects for robot processing. Clearly, GMF was a knowledge link between GM and Fanuc.*

Fanuc was the personal handiwork of Dr. Sieuemon Inaba, its founder and chief executive. In 1955, Fujitsu, the Japanese electronics and computer company, placed him in charge of a team of 500 engineers whose mission was to develop a factory automation business. Under Inaba's leadership, Fanuc became the world's leader in computerized numerical controls—electronic boxes that control the movement of machine tools such as lathes and milling machines. Fanuc was an ultra-workaholic company: 14-hour workdays were ordinary for managers and researchers. Inaba ran Fanuc with military precision. In fact, Fanuc and GM formed their venture within three months of their first contact. Although this pace of decision making was almost unheard of at GM, it was quite natural for Fanuc, where Inaba had installed a clock in the product development lab that ran at 10 times normal speed.

GM executives gave several reasons for joining forces with Fanuc. First, as the largest U.S. user of robots, GM bought about a third of all robots sold in the United States. These, along

---

* As is often the case, GMF served many of the purposes of a product link. The company, which would set up its headquarters and manufacturing facilities in Michigan, would have the exclusive right to sell robots made in Japan by Fanuc throughout North and South America, Australia, and New Zealand. In this way, GMF would help Fanuc increase its volume of operations and thereby make additional contributions to its fixed costs.

with tens of thousands of computers and numerical control units, were part of GM's high-tech manufacturing strategy. Second, GM was dissatisfied with some of its own robot vendors. Third, GM had developed an expertise in robotics and wanted to find a way to convert this knowledge into products and sell it. Fourth, GM was afraid it might lose some of its robotics personnel and technology to other robotics companies. Inaba joined with GM because he wanted to build Fanuc's robotics business. In particular, he felt limited by Japanese robot technology. He believed that U.S. and European firms were ahead of the Japanese in developing intelligent robots with visual functions, robots capable of walking around factory floors and offices on their own feet, and robots connected with CAD/CAM systems.

GMF development efforts were coordinated by meetings held four times a year and involving senior executives from GMF and Fanuc. Teams of engineers from Fanuc, GMF, and GM conducted individual projects. Some projects concentrated on hardware, aiming at developing smaller, more economical, and more specialized units. Others focused on programming and communications language. Perhaps the most extensive effort was the development of Karel, a programming language that linked GMF robots, vision systems, and other devices to both GMF and non-GMF products.

In creating GMF, its parents avoided the difficulties of trying to work together through a series of arm's-length market relationships. They were able to collaborate even though a merger of the two companies was impossible. Neither company had to rely wholly on its own resources for further development in robotics. They concentrated only on the particular projects that interested both parties. Their radically different company cultures could be kept largely separate and intact, while the project-driven interactions could be carefully monitored and managed. And, above all, key researchers and engineers from both companies could work together, day by day, in order to learn from each other, create adaptations of the technology and expertise that each had developed alone, and in so doing strengthen their capabilities and those of their partners.

The GMF example is instructive but somewhat limited. It does display two of the principal characteristics of knowledge links. GMF helped both partners broaden certain skills and capabilities, and it also created intimate working relationships among personnel from the parent organizations. GMF does not, however, display the two other characteristics of knowledge links. One is the way a company can use a multitude of knowledge links as part of an effort to transform its core capabilities. The other is the variety of knowledge partners from which a firm can choose.

TRANSFORMING CAPABILITIES THROUGH ALLIANCES

To understand these last two characteristics, it is necessary to take a strategic view of the many alliances GM and IBM created in the 1980s. Examining the risks, rationales, and structures of individual alliances is not enough. Such an approach results in scrupulous analysis of trees but little understanding of forests. It fails to answer a crucial question: how do all of a company's alliances relate to each other and how do they support and renew a firm's core capabilities? An answer requires an analysis of a company's strategy, its other alliances, changes in its core operations, and trends in its industry.

Viewed cumulatively rather than one at a time, the knowledge links created by GM and IBM in the 1980s were genuinely strategic. They were not simply product links, aimed at filling gaps in a product line or helping to cover fixed costs. Nor were they simply efforts to add a handful of new capabilities to the repertories of these two giants. Instead, IBM used a myriad of knowledge links as part of a larger effort to transform its traditional core capability of making and selling mainframe computers. GM began to use knowledge links with its suppliers, its workers and their union, and its dealers, as part of a bold, perilous effort to dramatically alter its capabilities for designing and manufacturing cars. IBM, in short, was trying to transform its products; GM, its operations.

The strategies of both firms were also preemptive: they aimed to change the terms of competition in their industries and tilt the playing field in their favor.[4] The 1990s will indicate whether GM and IBM succeed in their daring efforts; meanwhile, Niccolo Machiavelli's observation is pertinent to both firms: "There is nothing more difficult to plan, more doubtful of success, nor more dangerous to manage than the creation of a new order of things."[5]

IBM's Knowledge Links

Since the mid-1950s, IBM's core capability has been financing, designing, manufacturing, and selling mainframe computers. For most of this time, mainframes dominated the computer industry, and IBM dominated the mainframe business. As a result, it became one of the most profitable companies in the history of commerce. By the 1980s, however, the computer industry began to shift course dramatically and IBM's environment became less stable and more hostile.

Above all, IBM had to respond to the radical changes in the computer industry, which were driven by trends toward ever-cheaper computer power and toward larger, better-integrated networks. Kojii Kobayashi, the chairman of NEC, a major Japanese computer firm, described these developments by distinguishing between "point" and "space." Point represents the mainframe-dominated era in which all computerized data flowed to and from a single centralized machine. Space represents a future era in which networks of powerful local machines distribute data-processing capability throughout a company, a country, or the world. The shift from point to space gives a radically different answer to the question "What is a computer?" The old answer was: a solitary central-processing unit. The new answer: a computer is a network.

These developments gave rise to a surge of new entrants in the computer industry. They aggressively attacked the developing areas of the industry as well as its traditional market segments, including IBM's inner sanctum, the mainframe business. Moreover, entrants were not the only aggressors. Established computer companies, long accustomed to following in IBM's wake, were reinvigorated and emboldened by the prospect of competing against the giant on a new playing field with a new set of rules. Hundreds of companies were developing new capabilities that IBM might or would need to serve its customers. These capabilities took four basic forms: designing high-powered, customized computers for special tasks; using intimate knowledge of a customer's particular needs to write software for the customer; bringing state-of-the-art technology to market quickly in a rapidly changing and intensely competitive business; and using familiarity with customer requirements to design customized computer networks.

The transition from point to space reinforced old threats to IBM and created new ones. Computer buyers wanted to build networks using compatible hardware and software from a variety of suppliers. In computer jargon, they preferred open architecture to the proprietary systems of a single supplier. Almost every major computer company was offering customers an open architecture based on Unix, the operating system software that Bell Laboratories had developed in the early 1970s.[6] By 1987, AT&T had licensed Unix to 225 computer firms, including the two largest Japanese computer makers, Hitachi and Fujitsu, which both sold mainframes that ran Unix. For small specialized computer manufacturers trying to compete in niches against IBM or DEC, Unix offered a way to provide products that were compatible with and connected to a wide range of different computer systems. Some industry estimates suggested that nearly 25% of all computers in the world, as measured by dollar value, would use Unix by the end of 1991.[7]

In essence, Unix was accelerating the trend toward building ever more powerful minicomputers, workstations, and microcomputers and toward linking these machines in a vast communications network. It threatened to create an alternative computer standard to IBM's proprietary operating systems. A specter haunting IBM was the prospect of a loose, worldwide alliance of Unix-based manufacturers, including IBM's most daunting Japanese competitors as well as the growing number of Unix customers.

In response to this threat and to the growth of new capabilities throughout the industry, IBM created scores of knowledge links. Through them it hoped to secure access to and build new skills and, ultimately, to transform its basic capabilities. IBM fought the battle to survive and prosper on two principal fronts: in the United States, its largest market, and in Japan, where it could counterattack its Japanese adversaries in their home market.

In telecommunications, for example, IBM Japan created a series of collaborative endeavors with NTT, the Japanese telecommunications monopoly, which the government was gradually deregulating in the 1980s. The two companies worked together to develop hardware, software, and organizational capabilities in large-scale computer networks. IBM Japan also formed alliances with Mitsubishi, Japan's largest trading company, to create a joint satellite communications service in Japan and to design and sell equipment for information network services. As a trading company, Mitsubishi wanted to combine IBM's technological know-how with its own expertise in managing a global network of trading operations and customer relationships.[8]

Starting in the mid-1970s, IBM USA formed a series of alliances in the telecommunications business. One of its partners was MCI Communications. MCI was AT&T's major U.S. competitor in long-distance telephone services, and its market share was expected to climb from 10% in 1987 to nearly 14% by 1991. Through the deal, MCI gained credibility, customers, and access to a communications network that IBM was developing, while IBM strengthened its position in telecommunications by becoming a major shareholder in the industry's most important independent company. IBM and MCI engineers and managers collaborated on large communications projects for the government and for firms creating private networks. In the late 1980s, MCI decided to buy back IBM's 16% stake, but industry analysts expected the two companies to continue working closely together because of their complementary skills in computer equipment and communications lines.[9]

In the 1980s, IBM also formed an alliance with Rolm, one of the world's leading manufacturers of private branch exchanges (PBXs), which are, in effect, computers that switch telephone calls and data. IBM hoped that Rolm would provide it with capabilities to route data and voice communications within an information network. Rolm, on the other hand, hoped to benefit from the cash the IBM deal provided, from IBM's corporate relationships, and from IBM's capabilities and overseas marketing. The IBM-Rolm alliance was ultimately unsuccessful; IBM soon bought all of Rolm's shares and made it a subsidiary, and later IBM placed Rolm's operations in an alliance with Siemens. Despite the turbulence and frustrations, the alliances with Rolm and, later, with Siemens were a part of IBM's worldwide effort to build up its capabilities in telecommunications.

To develop applications software and other capabilities, IBM created scores of cooperative alliances. In Japan, it formed Nissan Systems Development with Nissan Motor to create applications software for basic research, product development, and manufacturing, particularly in automotive electronics. The Mitsubishi Bank and IBM Japan embarked on a joint venture to develop and sell software for Japanese banks. With Nippon Kokan, the second largest Japanese steel maker, IBM jointly developed an artificial intelligence system for planning steelmaking schedules. IBM Japan also worked with many of its newly created dealerships, such as liquor wholesalers and heating oil distributors, to develop specialized software that could be sold to them and to other companies in their businesses.[10]

In the United States, in the late 1980s, IBM USA created more than a dozen alliances—usually through minority equity investments—with companies that had expert capabilities in particular areas of software design. These included firms specializing in molecular simulation, image processing, insurance company transactions, management of large commercial projects, and software used to design software. Other new partners, such as a producer of signal converters for fiber optics communications, made hardware that would help IBM build customized networks. IBM's alliances also included a joint venture with Stephen Chen, one of the world's leading supercomputer designers; the creation and partial financing of Sematech, a consortium of U.S. semiconductor manufacturers; and an R&D

partnership with Motorola to improve semiconductor manufac-turing. Through these partnerships, IBM secured access to ca-pabilities developed by firms that competed, in effect, in niches within niches. The firms relied upon specialized areas of expertise that IBM lacked and did not intend to develop on its own, but that it needed to provide to some of its customers. Through the Sematech, Motorola, and supercomputer alliances, it aimed to strengthen its partners and work with them to create new capabilities.

Through this constellation of knowledge links, IBM was slowly transforming itself from a supplier of mainframe hard-ware into an international computer and telecommunications firm that could provide global companies, as well as smaller firms, with companywide networks for transmitting and processing voice, data, and images.[11] In essence, IBM was changing itself to adapt to and capitalize on the transition from point to space. Its scores of knowledge links were part of its effort to become efficiently global and, simultaneously, intensively local and re-sponsive. IBM could offer a company with worldwide operations, such as Nomura Securities or Ford Motor, customized hardware and software that linked all their desks, offices, machines, and factories around the world. IBM's national subsidiaries, like IBM Japan, could also rely upon their partners to offer the local offices of Nomura or Ford customized applications software and com-puter networks.

GM's Knowledge Links

Viewed one at a time, many of GM's alliances, like GMF Robotics, served to extend particular capabilities. Cumu-latively, however, they also contributed to most dramatic strategic changes at GM in the past half-century. Like IBM, GM has used a multitude of new alliances as part of a strategy of transformation. The alliances have given GM access to capabilities and pools of expertise that it needs, but that it chose not to invent or reverse engineer or develop on its own. GM's vast array of new alliances can appear confusing at first glance. Fortunately, a single effort—

the Saturn project—can introduce GM's new boundary arrangements and can provide a helicopter view of GM's effort to transform itself. Saturn and Saturn-like changes throughout GM also represent GM's bid to recapture leadership in the world automobile industry and to hold it well into the twenty-first century. In particular, GM threw down the gauntlet to Toyota, challenging it to venture forth from its redoubt in Toyota City and confront GM in North America, in a battle to be fought with capital and advanced technology.

The basic facts about the Saturn subsidiary, GM's sixth car division, are straightforward. In 1983, GM announced that it would spend $3.5 billion to create a compact car called Saturn, the first new GM nameplate since the introduction of Chevrolet in 1918. The Saturn plant, a new facility to be located in Spring Hill, Tennessee, would employ 6,000 workers and produce 500,000 cars a year, beginning in 1989. Because it would manufacture all the major car parts, the plant would include extensive foundry, machining, engine, and transmission assembly facilities, as well as metal stamping and final assembly operations. Parts and components imported from Japan would account for less than 1% of the cost of the Saturn, a dramatic shift from GM's reliance on car and parts suppliers in its portfolio of Asian alliances. In 1986, GM scaled down plans for Saturn because of capital constraints, halving its budget to about $1.7 billion. Its initial capacity would be 240,000 cars per year, and the first cars would be launched in the fall of 1990. In the early 1990s, GM would start a second construction phase to double Saturn's capacity.

What this brief overview does not make clear is that the Saturn project was hardly an ordinary car operation.[12] It was designed on a "clean sheet of paper" basis, so that its personnel could design, engineer, manufacture, distribute, and sell cars in pathbreaking ways. GM chairman Roger Smith announced:

> GM believes that what it is doing is potentially significant to anyone who operates a plant in any industry, anywhere in the United States, because

the leading-edge technologies that Saturn represents
could affect every one of them. And the improve-
ments that flow naturally from Saturn could ultimately dwarf past accomplishments and establish
U.S. industry, once again, as the leader in a new age
of almost cosmic industrial achievement.[13]

Martin Weitzman, a labor relations expert and economics professor at MIT, said that "if Saturn succeeds, you can
legitimately call it revolutionary."[14] *BusinessWeek* described Saturn as a "bid to do nothing short of revolutionizing automobile
manufacturing."[15] Saturn would draw on technology and skills
from within GM, from EDS and Hughes Aircraft (GM's major
high-tech acquisitions of the 1980s), from the many partnerships
already described in this chapter, and from a new set of knowledge
links with the UAW, with suppliers, and with dealers.

The alliances with the last three groups were a vital
part of the transformation GM sought to achieve. For the UAW,
Saturn represented a new era of collaboration. The project
marked the first time in GM history that the UAW had participated in GM corporate planning. In the words of president Owen
Beiber, the union would be a "full partner" in all of Saturn's
decision making, and "no decision could be reached without its
approval."[16] Saturn would be run by a strategic action council,
consisting of the project's president and staff and the top UAW
advisers. A "manufacturing action council," also including UAW
representatives, would oversee the day-to-day operations, and
work units—teams of 6 to 15 workers led by a UAW "coun-
cilor"—would perform manufacturing and assembly tasks.

Saturn sought to go beyond even NUMMI in encouraging participatory labor relations. GM had many motives
for pursuing this new relationship, but a crucial one involved
knowledge and capabilities. Toyota's approach to labor relations
succeeds, in part, because it motivates workers to develop thousands of ideas about ways of improving automobile manufacturing
and design. It thus makes practical use of the knowledge and
experience of the workers who make the cars and their compo-

nents. Toyota's approach also provides workers with incentives and opportunities to communicate what they know to the rest of the organization.

Moreover, Toyota-style manufacturing builds embedded knowledge at the individual and team levels. Its workers are cross-trained in a variety of skills. Hence, they can detect flaws in each other's work, suggest ways they can work together more effectively, and gradually develop higher levels of skill through experience and training. (At one GM plant, 30 cross-trained workers reduced warranty costs on suspension systems by 400% in a mere two years.) Finally, cross-training helped workers handle the increasingly complex, often computerized equipment on the factory floor. Saturn executives wanted every member of the organization to contribute steadily and vigorously to the creation and dissemination of knowledge. Saturn would succeed if the new partnership between GM, the UAW, and its workers could create a powerful information-sharing team. This approach departed radically from traditional, arm's-length, adversarial management-union relationships in the auto industry, and it sought to halt the decades-long trend toward deskilling automobile manufacturing and "dumbing down" the tasks it required of workers.

For similar reasons, at Saturn and at many other GM facilities, GM was seeking to create new collaborative relationships with its suppliers. In the past, GM had handled most of its suppliers by—in the words of one of its purchasing executives—"handing them our list of requirements and asking for a sealed bid." In effect, GM had practiced classical, arm's-length, market contracting. Many supplier relationships had been renewed on a year-to-year basis, and GM had often switched suppliers to secure lower prices. At Saturn, in contrast, supplier relations would be far more intimate and collaborative. One reason was the just-in-time system that Saturn was implementing. JIT requires deliveries on an hourly rather than a weekly or monthly basis and hence calls for close communication and coordination with suppliers. GM's managers said that Saturn would establish long-term relationships with suppliers that would meet its time and quality demands, rather than shop around each year for the lowest-cost supplier. Moreover, suppliers could achieve "preferred supplier" status. That meant GM would work with them on product development, soliciting ideas and assisting them with designs and component production. Like GM's relationship with the UAW, this effort enlisted suppliers in the creation and dissemination of new knowledge. Through close collaboration, GM and its suppliers would work to develop proprietary technology that would give GM distinctive advantages and to find ways to enable GM to use the technology quickly and efficiently. GM needed these advances badly, in part to recover from the cost-cutting and parts standardization efforts that had led to look-alike cars some analysts nicknamed "Oldsbuicadillacs."

GM developed its capabilities in data processing through a wide network of knowledge links with its computer and computer-related suppliers. Together, they worked to create what GM called its Manufacturing Automation Protocol (MAP). In the past, GM's computer suppliers had provided proprietary systems and hardware that could not communicate with each other or could do so only through complex, expensive interface devices. MAP asked the vendors to integrate their islands of computing and to help GM create a common communication network based on a nonproprietary language—the equivalent of asking hundreds of locomotive manufacturers to alter their products so they could all run on the same gauge track. To develop MAP, GM engaged in ongoing technical discussions with committees representing scores of hardware and software suppliers, ranging from giants like IBM and DEC to small hardware and software shops. These discussions are expected to last well into the 1990s, as the committees develop a succession of communication standards, each moving a step closer to full compatibility.

GM also made minority equity investments in small, high-tech companies—such as Automatix, View Engineering, Diffracto, and Robotic Vision Systems—that provided opportunities for its engineers to work with and learn from their counterparts about advanced automation technology and also gave GM and its partners the opportunity to collaborate in designing products for the auto industry. For example, in 1988, GM and Teknowledge announced that they had developed an expert system—an artificial intelligence software program that simulates the judgments of experts in a particular field—that would troubleshoot various types of machine tools, metal-cutting systems, and assembly machines. It could detect problems stemming from conditions such as bearing wear, unbalanced parts, and misalignment. At MIT's Media Lab, a multidisciplinary research center studying communications and computer technology, GM joined with the U.S. Defense Department on projects studying holography and human-machine interfaces.[17]

Finally, Saturn's planners wanted its distribution system to break down the arm's-length, highly contractual, often adversarial relations between GM and its dealers. Hence, Saturn would have its own franchise system and dealer organization. Most important, however, the franchise agreements stated specifically that the dealers were to be "partners" in Saturn's operations. They would be involved in decisions not only about dealerships but also about product planning. As with suppliers and workers, GM sought to shift to a new relationship in which it could learn from and work more closely with its dealerships.

CONCLUSION

This overview of the strategies of GM and IBM shows how they have used knowledge links to meet the challenges of embedded knowledge. At the simplest level, these alliances served as organizational devices to help them avoid the difficulties of trying to gain access to or create embedded knowledge through the traditional methods of market relationships, acquisitions, or going-it-alone. But knowledge links can make broader contributions. They can help a company extend its expertise in one or more directions. And, if a company is willing to act as boldly as GM and IBM have, they can contribute to a strategy through which it may be able to transform its core capabilities and perhaps even change the terms of competition in its industry.

How likely IBM and GM are to succeed in this transformation is far from certain. IBM's fortunes will depend on its
success at reducing costs and increasing its speed to market, on
the strength of whatever Unix coalition emerges, on the progress
of IBM's Japanese competitors, and on government regulation of
telecommunications in many countries around the world. But
IBM has built on a solid foundation: the communications networks that it has already created for some of the largest companies
in the world; its dominant, highly profitable mainframe business;
the prospect that many smaller companies, and even some government agencies, will accept its dominance in global networks;
and its efforts through a vast range of strategic alliances to learn
skills and capabilities that it did not have and make them available
to customers throughout the world.

GM faced other difficulties. It began creating a large
constellation of knowledge links at the same time as it was trying
to transform its internal operations. The company spent much
of the 1980s implementing and refining the most massive reorganization in 50 years. During the decade, GM also acquired
Hughes Aircraft, the world's leading defense electronics firm, and
Electronic Data Services, the world's leading systems integration
firm, in order to secure technology and skills that it hoped would
radically change its approach to auto making. GM paid a steep
price for these simultaneous changes. Costs rose at a time when
the intensively competitive U.S. market was limiting price in-
creases. As a result, in 1988 and 1989, GM earned negligible
profits on its North American auto operations. Worse, its GM-
10 cars—a new series of more stylish, higher-quality, mid-sized
cars—reached market late, well after Ford's Taurus and Sable
had made deep inroads in GM's market position.

The difficulties encountered by IBM and GM in the
late 1980s could easily lead to skepticism about the value of
knowledge links. This reaction, however, would be wrong. Many
of the most powerful and competitive Japanese companies, such
as Toyota and Matsushita, rely heavily upon knowledge links
with suppliers and labor unions. During its renaissance in the
1980s, Ford Motor relied on alliances in Japan and Korea, on

much closer and more cooperative ties with suppliers, and on a new partnership with workers and the UAW. Michael Porter's recent study of countries with internationally competitive industries concluded that a nation's successful firms are often linked together in "clusters." Within these, an assortment of mechanisms—various forms of knowledge links—promote the flow of knowledge among a wide range of organizations.[18]

In the cases of GM and IBM, efforts to look more closely at individual alliances and to trace their effects are riddled with difficulty. Many GM and IBM alliances are quite recent, so final judgments must wait several years. Moreover, both companies are in the midst of what may prove to be historic transformations—or perhaps declines—and they are changing in response to many factors, not just to alliances. Consider the cases in which productivity, absenteeism, and quality measures indicate than GM has created a successful, collaborative relationship with the UAW—at Saturn, for example, or at the Chevrolet plant that makes Corsicas and Berrettas. How much credit goes to what GM learned from its alliance with Toyota, how much to internal efforts beginning with the Quality of Work Life program in the early 1970s, and how much to the shift toward more cooperative industrial relations underway in many American companies? To the extent that GM has failed to change its labor relations quickly enough, how much of its tardiness comes from not knowing how managers can help their organization learn new capabilities from an alliance, and how much from the traditional adversarial relationship between GM and its workers? Even ostensibly precise quantitative measures fail to tell much of a story. For example, GM's sales of cars made with its Asian allies have fallen short of initial targets. Why? Because of the alliances themselves, the wrong choice of partners, or the mid-1980s market shift toward larger cars? Or was it because Pontiac dealers earned higher margins for selling large cars like Bonnevilles and Grand Prix's rather than the subcompact LeMans's made by the Daewoo alliance?

Moreover, the question of comparison makes assessments of alliances even more difficult. Alliances are often criticized as unstable because many of them last only several

years. But compared to what? Are partnerships less stable, in
general, than organizational arrangements inside firms? In the
1980s, General Electric created roughly 100 strategic alliances;
some prospered, others failed, and many needed redesign during
their lives. But in the same period, General Electric reorganized
itself dramatically, reduced total employment by 100,000, and
bought and sold scores of businesses. GM and IBM both over-
hauled their internal operations and organization in the 1980s,
and then made a multitude of corrections and refinements. During this period of organizational earthquakes and aftershocks
inside GE, GM, and IBM, were the core operations of the companies less turbulent than their alliances?

Even if some of the alliances created by U.S. companies in recent years have proved difficult to manage, it does
not follow that companies should avoid them. Historical comparison is also important. Early in this century, American firms
spent decades adopting, refining, and learning to manage the
multidivisional form of organization that Du Pont, Sears, GM,
and a few other companies had invented. In contrast, the U.S.
experiment with alliances has been brief. From the perspective
of a twenty-first century historian, product and knowledge links
may represent only the initial phases of a decades-long effort to
find new and more flexible forms of organization suited to knowledge-driven, global markets.

While it is difficult to foresee and assess the ultimate
effects of these changes, one conclusion is quite firm: the pace
and magnitude of the changes in GM's and IBM's boundaries
have been astonishing. Ultimately, the success of GM and IBM
will depend on many factors, and not simply on the contributions
that knowledge links can make. How much these alliances contribute to the two companies' efforts to secure embedded knowledge, extend their capabilities, and transform themselves will
depend on how well these alliances are managed and how quickly
these longtime citadels can learn from close relationships with
outside organizations.

CHAPTER 6

Managing Alliances

Peter Drucker has observed that strategy must ultimately degenerate into work. A strategy that utilizes alliances is, like any other, no better than its implementation.[1] Its success depends, in part, on how well the alliances are managed. But what does management consist of? Managing alliances, particularly knowledge links, is at bottom a process of learning, creating, sharing, and controlling knowledge. As executives manage the boundaries of their firms, they are determining when and how knowledge and skills will move into and out of their organizations. To succeed, they frequently must break down the walls around their firms and teach their organization to learn in new, often uncomfortable and threatening ways.

Creating and managing alliances is an unnatural act for many American managers. Intellectually and intuitively, they believe that firms are best run as citadels. For decades, powerful forces have led them to strip-mine knowledge and skills from many of their crucial ongoing relationships. Workers' tasks were deskilled, often to the point of mind-numbing repetition; labor unions were treated as adversaries with whom it was dangerous to share in-depth knowledge about a business; government was seen as another antagonist, whose regulators, antitrust enforcers, and other meddlers were best kept at arm's-length; and suppliers and buyers often communicated little more to each other than price specifications and delivery dates. Yet American executives did become adept at managing knowledge *within* their firms' boundaries. As Chapter 4 showed, companies are repositories of embedded knowledge. Inside them, information, technology, rumors, cost data, plans, judgments about personnel, trial balloons, and other sorts of knowledge move within complex social and administrative networks.

Indeed, the best starting point for understanding how to manage alliances is an examination of the factors that encourage or impede the acquisition, communication, and creation of knowledge within an organization. These factors do not fit neatly together in a formula, and their relative weight varies from situation to situation. They include: a clear sense of a project's objectives; incentives to share and build knowledge and skills; the right basic resources and capabilities; a champion or leadership team with strong personal commitment to the endeavor's success; a sense of teamwork and purpose among participants at all levels; encouragement, albeit within limits, to experiment, fail, and try again; a sense of trust among the individuals and groups expected to contribute knowledge, skills, and resources; and support from senior management.

In short, what matter are leadership, trust, and commitment. These commodities are often scarce inside companies, because of politics, bureaucracy, and other impediments. In alliances, the challenges are even greater. Over time, partners may come to disagree on an alliance's purpose and objectives; in a world of fluctuating exchange rates and proliferating knowledge, this can happen quickly. Even if the partners have complementary capabilities, they may be reluctant to share them, particularly if the companies are or could become competitors. The "not-invented-here" mentality can lead each partner to undervalue the capabilities the other brings to an alliance. Trust and commitment are imperiled when organizations with different cultures must communicate and work together. This problem is especially serious when the allies have a long history of antagonism, which is the case for many American companies and their suppliers, workers, labor unions, dealers, and the government. Partners may also need to reconcile different management systems—for accounting, compensation, promotions, and reporting. Finally, strong leadership may be less likely to emerge in a joint enterprise for which two or more bosses are ultimately responsible; such arrangements violate Napoleon's maxim that one bad general does better than two good ones.

Alliances that overcome these challenges can help companies prosper in a world of knowledge-intensive competition. But under what conditions is this likely to happen? The experiences, either successful or disappointing, of the firms examined in this book, as well as experiences reported in other studies of joint ventures and cooperative R&D suggest what these conditions are. They can be created by managers with different skills and styles—as long as, ultimately, the basic conditions are met. When this happens, the dice are loaded in favor of success.

The first condition is that managers considering an alliance must have a clear, strategic understanding of their company's current capabilities and the capabilities it will need in the future. In their haste to consummate a deal that fills an urgent need, managers can easily leave this condition unmet. As a result, they may commit their company to an alliance that makes sense as a discrete deal but causes strategic damage. A product link might, for example, provide a company with a product it needs at a very low cost. Yet the partnership may take the pressure off managers and engineers to build the capabilities to develop similar products. The deal could also open new markets and teach crucial skills to the partner, thereby spawning a competitor.

In a world of knowledge-driven competition and fleeting product-based advantages, firms must be understood as pools of embedded knowledge and capabilities. This, not plants or cash or even patented technology, is their fundamental asset. A firm's core knowledge, capabilities, and skills can be identified through questions like these: Which individuals have the craftsman-like knowledge, born of special talent and particular experience, that sets them apart from their counterparts in competing firms? Which teams and groups "know" how to do things or make things better, faster, or more efficiently than their competitors? What are the crucial links, formal and informal, through which the company orchestrates these pools of individual and small-group talent? And what relationships with external parties are vital conduits for bringing new skills and capabilities into the company?

Looking to the future, the central questions are: What knowledge does a company need to meet its long-term strategic goals? Which capabilities—*not* necessarily which products—will give it an advantage over its competitors three to five years hence?[2] In a world of globalized knowledge, few firms are permanently powerful. Risks to a firm's capabilities can be uncovered by asking: What is the half-life of the core capabilities of a company? Which competitors—tiny startup firms, established firms, even nations—are aiming to replicate or improve on these capabilities and the products or services that they make possible?

Sustained strength is strength continually renewed. It rests upon the ability to create and replenish knowledge and capabilities—through a unique combination of internal efforts, market transactions, mergers and acquisitions, and product and knowledge links. Embedded knowledge is especially useful to firms, since it buys them time in which they can further build skills and reap profits for reinvestment in better technology, customer support, new products, and so forth. Embedded knowledge also gives firms more bargaining chips for negotiating alliances, and it helps attract a wider set of prospective partners. GM's North American distribution network, the bundle of skills and capabilities that Toyota has perfected in its Toyota City operations, and Fanuc's prowess at designing and manufacturing robots have opened doors to many possible relationships for each firm and have strengthened their hands in bargaining.

The second condition is that managers must consider a wide range of possible alliances. Alliances can greatly expand the opportunities managers have to build their companies' core capabilities. When managers consider possible alliances, they have three pivotal decisions to make. The first is the choice of a *partner.* As this study has shown, a firm may choose any type of organization, at home or overseas, as a partner. GM's and IBM's remarkable collections of partners link them with competitors, suppliers of parts and components, the UAW, the Media Lab at MIT, and government bodies here and abroad.

The second choice is deciding which *activities* the cooperative endeavor will undertake. IBM's and GM's new relationships show that all of the classical business functions can be performed collaboratively—including marketing, manufacturing, R&D, and finance, as well as decisions about pricing, capacity, product lines, and even strategy. The third choice establishes the *form* of the relationship. Both IBM and GM have relied upon joint ventures, licensing agreements, minority equity investments, and forums for technical collaboration, as well as less formal, more flexible arrangements based on long-standing relationships and mutual trust.

Just as DNA, the biochemical building block of life, combines into myriad forms, so these three deceptively simple decisions can be made in an unlimited variety of ways, creating relationships between organizations that range from loose and tenuous links to close, intricate, time-honored ties. In making these decisions, managers can act boldly. One example is the multiplicity of alliances that IBM Japan has created. These transformed it quickly and dramatically from a large IBM overseas subsidiary into a true Japanese enterprise group. GM's alliances in Korea are another example. They are not simply tie-ups with companies in the Daewoo Group. Like Japan in the 1950s and 1960s, Korea in the 1980s pursued a strategy of international development orchestrated by government planners, its Ministry of Finance, major banks, and the heads of the conglomerate groups that dominate the Korean economy. Daewoo was among the most important of these groups, and its businesses competed in all the strategic sectors of the Korean economy. Through the Daewoo relationship, GM had, in effect, a loose partnership with "Korea Incorporated."

The third condition is that before committing their company to an alliance, managers must scrutinize the values, commitment, and capabilities of prospective partners. In order to assess a possible partner's values and culture, a manager must be aware of many varied and often subtle factors. Companies, like other social communities, develop norms of behavior, symbols, and ways of interpreting the environment. They resemble villages, which seem similar to a traveler passing quickly through, but which are idiosyncratic and sometimes even inexplicable to those who stop and stay a while. Complex cultural differences distinguish firms, not only in the same country, but even in the same city and the same industry. Some crucial questions that managers must ask are: Does the company (or university laboratory or government body or labor union) make decisions in a centralized or decentralized way? What vision of the future is its leaders pursuing? Do its managers seem open or secretive? How do they treat each other? Does the prospective partner seem to value internal cooperation? What relative values does it place on technology, marketing, product quality, and financial results? What attitude toward risk do its past actions imply? What kind of company do its customers, suppliers, and competitors think it is? There is no checklist that guarantees coverage of all relevant factors, but the answers to questions like these help managers to sketch a composite picture of a potential ally. The more closely the two companies' values match, the better a partnership's prospects.

Assessment of a possible ally's capabilities also requires a strategic perspective. An attractive partner for a knowledge link has a combination of products, knowledge, technology, capabilities, financial strength, and talent. Moreover, its strategy *commits it* to use or develop these capabilities in an alliance, rather than through independent efforts, mergers, or market transactions. By determining the prospective partner's strategic intent, managers can find out how serious the partner is about the alliance and what caliber of personnel and resources it is likely to commit; with this information, they will be better able to protect their firm's interests. Working with a prospective partner on a small preliminary project is often a safe way to get a clearer sense of the other party's culture and capabilities before creating a full-scale alliance. In the end, a promising ally should show depth of capabilities and commitment, not just capital or the capacity to produce a single product cheaply today. Such an ally will be able to adapt and persevere when technology, exchange rates, markets, and government policies change, as they surely will.

  The fourth condition is that managers must understand the risks of opportunism, knowledge leaks, and obsolescence. The question of opportunism and self-interest is especially pressing when partners want to create new knowledge and capabilities. Dealings between companies engaged in knowledge-intensive competition are unlikely to be guided solely by harmony and goodwill. The race to develop knowledge and capabilities is just as intense, conflict-ridden, and plagued by opportunism as were past battles for crucial resources such as fertile land, capital, deposits of natural resources, or the trade routes connecting Renaissance city-states. Often, the partners are competing with each other—for profits, market share, resources, and knowledge—at the same time as they cooperate. In other cases, they may become competitors in the future.

  When a firm forms a partnership with a strong, successful competitor—as GM did with Toyota—this problem can become acute. How much will a powerful partner be willing to commit to an alliance if it is competing against its ally in other markets? Common sense and business experience both suggest that the general answer is, "No more than necessary." Toyota did not join forces with GM out of an altruistic desire to aid the firm that was among its most dangerous adversaries. Rather, Toyota joined NUMMI at a moment of vulnerability. Rising protectionist barriers in the United States were threatening its strategy of exporting aggressively from its Japanese production base. Toyota's competitors, Nissan and Honda, had much more experience than Toyota in managing overseas operations—because of Honda's experience in the motorcycle business and because both Nissan and Honda had been forced overseas by Toyota's strength in the domestic market. But in the early 1980s, Toyota had no experience with U.S. workers and labor unions, U.S. suppliers and truckers, or managing a large overseas operation, and its efforts to form an alliance with Ford had failed. NUMMI provided Toyota with the opportunity to learn about American business, and consequently it agreed to a joint venture with GM, even though it knew it was providing GM with a badly needed apprenticeship in Toyota's skills and management practices.

Toyota drove a hard bargain. The car that NUMMI first assembled was neither new nor stylish nor technologically sophisticated, but a vehicle Toyota had already been making and selling in Japan for several years. In the jargon of Detroit, the Chevrolet Nova was an "econobox," a small, fuel-efficient, well-made, unobtrusive vehicle. Also, Toyota permitted GM to sell only a four-door vehicle, keeping the two-door hatchback for itself. The latter car, the Corolla FX, sold successfully through Toyota dealerships without the financial incentives of several hundred dollars per car that GM offered with the Nova by 1987. In addition, the major components of the car, including the drive train, were made in Toyota City, so Toyota captured the margins and scale economies of their manufacture and kept their engineering and production away from GM's gaze.

Alliances, especially knowledge links, create the risk that knowledge and capabilities will flow to partners in unintended and harmful ways, through the actions of technicians or managers who are several levels below the executives responsible for an operation. In most cases, knowledge and capabilities do not migrate because a firm's partners are devious or predatory.[3] Rather, many of the relationships described in this book have been created expressly to combine the capabilities and knowledge of two firms. This means that each partner is expected to learn a certain amount about the other's capabilities and that channels of communication have been opened between them.

Knowledge links, managed carelessly, can become knowledge leaks. Over the years, the little brother in an alliance can outgrow and even dominate the older sibling. For example, in the 1960s, Honeywell relied on NEC to sell simple computers in Japan and to supply basic components. The relationship provided easy profits for Honeywell and an opportunity to fully exploit the sales potential of its older technology. As time passed, however, NEC's capabilities grew—by dint of its own efforts and through what it learned from its partners, including Honeywell. Ultimately, NEC became the dominant partner in its relationship with Honeywell. Its computer division was by far the larger of the two, and some of its technology was among the most advanced in the world. NEC became the principal hardware supplier to a three-way joint venture in which the other partners were Honeywell and France's Group Bull—an arrangement that most industry analysts regarded as a Honeywell retreat from the computer business.

Risks such as these are not reasons to shun alliances. Inevitably, a company will strengthen its partner—the ally would not have decided to join a partnership without the prospect of gain. GM strengthened Isuzu, Suzuki, and Daewoo by selling their cars through its North American dealer network. As with any business risk, the key questions are whether the risks have been assessed accurately, whether they are justified by the possible benefits, and whether they can be managed, or better still, reduced. For years, the Big Three U.S. auto firms underestimated the risks posed by their Japanese adversaries. GM may have underestimated the risks that Toyota would learn more from NUMMI than it would learn—because it was run by Toyota managers who were *forced* to learn to work with American workers, suppliers, and labor unions—and the risk that Toyota would deploy what it learned more quickly than GM by transferring its new skills to its Greenfield, Kentucky, plant. Hence, an important part of assessing a partnership's risks is asking how dangerous and how likely the worst-case scenario is. What are the chances that a partner will garner key knowledge and rapidly exploit it? How much damage would this cause?

The fifth condition is avoiding undue dependence on alliances. Alliances, in general, should be ways of supplementing and improving a firm's embedded knowledge, not substitutes for internal development. GM limited its dependence on its Asian allies through its Saturn project, which was an attempt to independently replenish the knowledge and capabilities crucial to its business.

Companies can also reduce dependence by being extremely cautious about alliances with competitors or alliances involving its core capabilities. British Prime Minister Palmerston said that Britain had no permanent friends or permanent enemies, only permanent interests. A firm's foremost interest must be in safeguarding and strengthening its core knowledge and skills.[4] (Sometimes, a weak firm has no choice but to enter a perilous relationship. Its executives should at least have their eyes open as they do so.) Both GM and IBM have followed this guideline in forming their new relationships. None of IBM's partnerships involved the manufacture, design, or sale of mainframe computers, which were its core skills. Furthermore, when IBM sought to link its personal computers with other computers and mainframes in large networks, it reduced its dependence on outside suppliers of parts and components. The PS/2 System is dramatically different—except for its software, which is designed by Microsoft, IBM's longtime ally, the system is proprietary. IBM designs and manufactures its crucial components in highly automated, wholly owned, and carefully guarded facilities.

GM considered but ultimately rejected a joint venture with EDS. If a joint effort with EDS had produced a breakthrough—new knowledge about automating automotive design, for example—then EDS, an extremely aggressive, market-oriented company, could have moved quickly to commercialize its new knowledge, possibly taking it to Ford, Chrysler, and other GM competitors. "Not-to-compete" clauses and other legal arrangements might have contained the problem, but enforcing such agreements is often costly and time-consuming, and it is ultimately frustrating when the knowledge at issue has already escaped. By owning EDS and Hughes Aircraft, GM could control the pace and direction of the flow of new knowledge. It secured ultimate control of both firms by owning them, thereby gaining assurance that the skills and knowledge it created through its joint efforts with each would be sold to other firms at a time and in a manner of GM's choosing.

When alliances do involve core capabilities, whether directly or indirectly, executives must guard against shifts in the balance of power, maneuvers by other parties, and the expropriation of vital knowledge or capabilities. Managing a firm's boundaries involves carefully monitoring all of a company's relationships for such dangers. A firm that has large-scale, complex relationships with another organization should assign a single executive to be "gatekeeper." The gatekeeper is responsible for overseeing all dealings between the organizations.[5]

Finally and paradoxically, a company can sometimes reduce its dependence on an alliance either by creating several similar alliances or by seeking to be the senior partner in the relationship. Toyota and Daewoo provided GM with different versions of the same product: high-quality, low-cost small cars. Toyota exercises hegemonic influence over its family of suppliers. It usually buys a large fraction of their output, often helps finance them, provides equipment and managerial advice, and sometimes lends its executives to them. Above all, it has integrated their production operations, intricately and intimately, with its assembly operations through JIT.

The sixth condition is that a company's alliances must be structured and managed like separate companies. Even if managers deal successfully with opportunistic partners, excessive dependence, and knowledge leaks, they face another set of challenges once an alliance has been established. These are the challenges of managing the myriad day-by-day and month-by-month details of successful cooperation.

The list of these challenges is lengthy.[6] Partners' accounting systems, compensation practices, management styles and culture sometimes differ significantly. The fact that a joint activity inevitably has two bosses—or more, depending on how many parents it has—can complicate and slow decision making. Even if one of the partners is given full responsibility for the day-to-day management of the operation, the parents must agree on major decisions. Special circumstances can add other difficulties. GM's dealings with its Asian partners were also complicated by antitrust scrutiny in the United States. The FTC required that Toyota and GM keep detailed logs describing discussions and transactions between the two companies. None of GM's other relationships were subject to this degree of scrutiny, but several of them required lengthy meetings with the FTC or the Antitrust Division of the Justice Department, as well as continuing reports on the ventures.

In order to overcome these challenges, managers should design an alliance as if they were establishing a separate company. An alliance should be a sphere of activity with an explicit mission and specific performance objectives, a timetable for their achievement, its own resources and control systems, and personnel with a sense of loyalty and commitment to the alliance's success. It should have clear guidance on what technology and know-how will be contributed to the alliance, what will remain proprietary, and what administrative mechanisms will resolve questionable cases. Through such arrangements managers can work closely with personnel from other organizations without risking the loss of knowledge and capabilities that would imperil the firm's strategic interests. In the creation of these unique, often fragile, minicompanies, painstaking attention to detail is crucial. In the phrase of architect Mies van der Rohe, "God resides in the details."

The managers of an alliance and the executives of their parent companies need to know what technological, financial, and competitive aims the alliance is intended to achieve. They should set clear milestones and performance measures so that everyone can assess its progress. The mission statement should also set clear limits on the partnership's activities. Can some of its activities overlap with those of a parent? Can it compete with its parent organizations? If so, in what markets? Of course, changes in market conditions and in the strategies of the parent companies, along with the trial-and-error approach inevitable in new endeavors and the constant proliferation of knowledge, preclude absolute clarity about an alliance's mission. As a result, some important details will have to be "filled in later." Hence, an alliance should include mechanisms—some formally specified in the initial contracts and others emerging only as the endeavor progresses—for resolving these issues as they arise. Moreover, the basic mission will have to be reviewed and updated by its parents, perhaps every three to five years. These reviews also provide occasions for firms to consider whether to expand their collaboration further. IBM Japan and NTT have gradually added joint ventures and other collaborative efforts to their initial alliance. Since 1971, GM and Isuzu have added partnerships in Great Britain and several developing countries.

Like an independent business, an alliance should be managed in a way that gives its personnel strong incentives to work for the success of the partnership, not merely of the parents. Successful relationships specify authority and roles. The parties involved know who is responsible for what, and measurement systems assess the performance of the joint effort. Moreover, one partner should, in most cases, have day-to-day operating responsibility for managing the alliance. Studies of one common form of collaboration, joint ventures, have found that this approach raises the chances of success. A recent managerially oriented study concluded that "the more 'shared' the management of a venture promises to be, the more difficult it will be to manage. . . . joint ventures in which both parents are heavily involved managerially have a much higher failure rate than those in which one or the other dominates."[7]

Each party should assign managers, engineers, and other personnel who are committed to making the venture work. And, beyond good intentions, they need the right skills. Each party tends to judge the other's commitment by the caliber of personnel assigned to the joint endeavor. Once assigned, crucial personnel should not be quickly rotated out of the alliance and back to the parent company. Fledgling enterprises need stability and the sharing or creation of embedded knowledge requires close, long-term, apprentice-like efforts.

If possible, a partnership should begin with small trial efforts at collaboration, so the parties can see whether their two cultures are sufficiently compatible and whether "champions" emerge on both sides—that is, managers with appropriate skills who are personally committed to making the venture work. At bottom, cooperative arrangements are not fundamentally links between one firm and another, nor do they connect firms and labor unions or firms and government agencies. Such abstractions do not exist, and they cannot have relationships with each other. Only individuals and small groups can. Hence, the success of a collaboration depends on whether specific individuals in separate organizations can work together and accomplish joint tasks.

The seventh condition is that the partners must come to trust each other. The importance of efforts to build trust is hard to overestimate. When managers are asked what matters most to successful alliances, they say consistently and with conviction that trust and open communication are indispensable.[8] Openness is paramount in knowledge links because much of what the parties are trying to learn from each other or create together is so difficult to communicate. It is often embedded in a firm's practices and culture, and it can only be learned through working relationships that are not hampered by constraints.

When two competitors join forces, as in the case of GM and Toyota, the problem of trust becomes even more troublesome. Managers on each side know how to treat competitors: with caution and suspicion. Employees are naturally inclined to hold their cards close to their chest, limiting collaboration with their partner. Every alliance is a unique, sometimes fragile, managerial and economic enterprise, with inescapable difficulties, errors, and surprises that can fester and swell into divisive issues. If an alliance encounters difficulty, partners can easily make scapegoats of each other. Mistrust, whatever its origins, breeds inflexibility. Studies have confirmed that when the parents of a joint venture trust each other, they are more inclined to grant substantial autonomy to managers, enabling them to respond more quickly to problems and opportunities and thereby raising the venture's chances of success.[9] The parties in a collaborative relationship are dependent on each other. Hence, the promotions, bonuses, and careers of the managers involved depend on the performance of the outside parties, with whom they have no prior experience and whose values and culture may differ radically from their own. In such situations, parties that do not trust each other are likely to create elaborate systems for running the joint endeavor, monitoring each other, and adjudicating disputes. Bureaucracy is a costly substitute for trust.

After an alliance is created, managers on both sides should expect to spend a great deal of time trying to make the relationship flourish. Ideally, the parties will begin working together on tasks at which they are likely to succeed. Then, rather than blame each other for frustrations and failures that often occur when initial tasks prove too difficult, both sides will grow more confident about the future. Moreover, the learning process, in organizations as in the world at large, usually takes place through a long series of small steps. The accumulation of small successes will reinforce this process.

The eighth condition is that managers must change their core operations and traditional organizations so that they will be open to learning from alliances. Successful alliances also depend upon the right relationship between the partnership and the organizations that create it. Consider, for example, a company that wants to create a knowledge link with a supplier so that the firms can work jointly to develop and test components for a new generation of products. The relationship will probably fail if the buyer does not change its procurement practices. The classic clerk with a green eyeshade who sends out purchase orders twice a year and chooses the lowest bidder cannot be the focal point of a knowledge-driven relationship with suppliers. Instead there must be collaboration among research, engineering, and marketing people from both the buyer and the supplier.

GM and its Asian partners created several organizational structures to manage their relationships.[10] For Isuzu and Suzuki, GM stationed personnel in Tokyo to facilitate their dealings with Chevrolet. These included marketing, manufacturing, and engineering consultants, as well as planners, procurement and distribution managers, and industry analysts. At the Daewoo Motor Company, GM was represented by a career executive who lived in Korea and served as executive president of the Daewoo Motor Company and its joint representative director. Roughly two-thirds of GM's Japanese suppliers had sales offices in the United States. Their representatives called on individual GM divisions and could summon engineering support, either from the United States or from Japan. At the same time, GM units like Delco and Harrison Radiator based managers in Japan to help coordinate relationships. GM also created a separate organization called Overseas Components Activities (OCA) that served as a bridge between divisions and its Japanese suppliers.

Even with such administrative arrangements firmly in place, a company can face difficulty in getting its own organization to take new, affiliated companies and their products seriously. Often, the cause is the not-invented-here syndrome. In other cases, functional personnel on both sides of a relationship complain about the division of labor and opportunities, saying that activities or investment funds were being diverted to a partner or to a joint venture rather than being given to them. The creation of a partnership is often viewed as evidence that some members of an organization have failed to perform as they should. Even when there are no clearly defined losers, collaboration may nevertheless bear the aura of failure or defeat. When GM linked itself with Toyota, it was conceding that Toyota—which two decades earlier had been mocked in Detroit for making tiny vehicles called Toyopets—could now teach it important lessons.

How seriously each partner views a relationship also depends upon the market conditions it faces. When demand for a company's products is strong, its alliances are not given high priority, since they do not seem to fill an urgent need. When demand is weak, personnel and managers tend to concentrate almost exclusively on fixing their own company's problems, and they pay less attention to distant overseas relationships. Only when demand falls into some intermediate zone are these relations taken completely seriously.

Companies must sometimes be willing to modify initial arrangements if they are to get the full benefit of the knowledge and capabilities of their partner. To its credit, IBM modified its relationship with Rolm several times—from partial equity ownership to full ownership of an independent subsidiary to integration in IBM's operations—before abandoning the effort. In contrast, GM has been criticized for failing to create organizational arrangements that would help it learn from NUMMI. In 1986, an MIT report concluded that the plant tours, videotapes, and manuals GM relied upon had conveyed only "a very partial understanding of NUMMI's procedures."[11] This suggested GM had failed to appreciate that learning and communicating embedded knowledge is far more difficult than passing along migratory knowledge.

GM's experience with efforts to transfer knowledge and capabilities led one of its executives to specify 10 steps crucial for success. They were:

1. Involve prospective users up front.
2. Encourage users to participate in the development of the technology.
3. Apply the new technology to a few critical problems before attempting to transfer it.
4. Package the technology so it is accessible to users.
5. Provide formal training in using the new technology.
6. Follow up to determine the effectiveness of the transfer process.
7. Provide users with the opportunities to meet collectively and share their experiences with the technology.
8. Do not rely solely on written reports to sell technology.
9. Be willing to provide resources such as people, time, and money to sell the technology.
10. Consider transferring people along with the technology.[12]

The final condition is that alliances must be led, not just managed. Even when it is done brilliantly, organizational design and attention to administrative detail alone cannot ensure the success of an alliance. Through words and actions, senior executives must clearly communicate the purpose, importance, and legitimacy of each alliance. They also need to set personal examples of commitment, patience, and flexibility, in order to

show how concerned they are that the relationship succeed. A
sense of urgency about taking advantage of alliances is particularly
important in firms that have managed themselves as citadels in
the past. Critics of GM's use of its Asian alliances often refer to
GM's decades-long tradition of concentrating on building large
cars for the North American market in fully owned North American facilities. IBM faces similar difficulties in shifting attention
away from its long-established focus on building mainframes and
selling them to large corporations.

Flexibility goes hand in hand with patience. Some
executives and many middle-level personnel have ideas about
strategy that are far too rigid for the fluid, knowledge-driven,
competition-driven world of alliances. The alliance strategies of
GM and IBM did not spring full-blown from the minds of corporate strategists. Rather, GM's strategy for dealing with the diffusion of small car know-how and IBM's strategy for dealing with
the migration of technology for personal computers reflected the
turbulence of a time when knowledge was being created at an
accelerating pace and was migrating in surprising directions. In
what Peter Drucker has called the "age of discontinuity," strategy
cannot be the equivalent of engineering blueprints conceptualized at one point and then cast in bronze forever. Strategy is the
evolution of a central idea over a long period of trial and error.
It is a pattern of decisions that evolves over time, under the aegis
of a few broad central objectives.

CHAPTER 7

Conclusion

What does the future hold? How will the strategies of firms evolve in response to the forces of knowledge? What changes may occur in the work of managers or in public policy? If the recent trends continue, the consequences may be dramatic. Consider how much has changed during the careers of Roger Smith and John Akers, chairmen of GM and IBM in the 1980s.

In 1949, Smith drove his Ford to a GM office in Detroit. By the day's end, he had a job as a general accounting clerk—he was a foot soldier in the most powerful industrial citadel in history.[1] GM had triumphed over Ford in the 1920s. It emerged from the Great Depression as the manufacturer of 40% of the cars sold in the United States. During World War II, GM became the nation's largest producer of war materiels. In the 1950s and 1960s, GM's wealth and gigantic earnings stream rendered the company independent of financial markets. The ethos of its self-perpetuating hierarchy of executives was summarized in the famous words of GM's president, Charles Wilson, in 1953: "What's good for General Motors is good for the country, and what's good for the country is good for General Motors." An extraordinary system of fortifications defined and defended GM's boundaries. Inside the firm were the vast assets owned by GM shareholders and controlled by its hierarchy of executives and managers. In 1966, GM stated bluntly that "unified ownership for coordinated policy control of all of its operations throughout the world is essential for its effective performance as a worldwide corporation."[2]

John Akers joined IBM as a sales trainee in 1960, when it was still a fairly small company with sales of less than

148   THE KNOWLEDGE LINK

$2 billion. Nine years later, however, when Akers was a branch manager in New York City, IBM implemented—with its 360 computer series—the most successful business strategy in history, as measured by the creation of shareholder wealth. Like GM, IBM prized its autonomy and built itself into an enormous, independent, industrial stronghold. It made few acquisitions, preferring to lure scientists away from universities and competitors and invest in its own controlled research and development. The company manufactured all of the essential components for its products. When possible, it avoided dependence on external capital, instead funding the next generation of products with the cash it got by leasing the current generation.

By the mid-1980s, however, Smith and Akers no longer presided over traditional citadels, but the central cores of worldwide webs of product and knowledge links. In fact, their boundary relationships were even more blurred and complex than this study of their automobile and computer businesses has shown. The business of GM's EDS subsidiary, for example, is designing, installing, and operating computer systems. EDS personnel work intimately with customers and with other computer makers and software designers, which, as subcontractors to EDS, provide specialized hardware and software. Through Hughes Aircraft, GM is involved in the symbiotic relationship with the Department of Defense commonly called "Pentagon Capitalism." Even some of GM's tiny partners had complex relationships with other firms. Teknowledge, a designer of artificial intelligence software products, had a handful of important customers, including GM, Procter & Gamble, Nynex, Elf Aquitaine, and FMC, and each of them owned 6–8% of Teknowledge's shares.

In all likelihood, as the forces of knowledge further intensify in Europe, the GM and IBM confederations will grow even larger and more complex during the 1990s. Through alliances and wholly owned operations, American and Japanese firms are bringing additional technology and capabilities to Western Europe. They want to take advantage of the large market that will emerge as European countries eliminate barriers. Many firms fear, however, that a Fortress Europe will exclude exports from the rest of the world. European companies, anticipating heightened competition, are expanding R&D and sourcing technology from around the world. In early 1990, Daimler-Benz and the Mitsubishi Group announced that they would pursue "intensive cooperation" among their automotive, electronics, aerospace, and other businesses. The potential range of joint endeavors was enormous: Daimler-Benz was the largest company in West Germany, with sales of nearly $50 billion, while the Mitsubishi Group of companies had sales of roughly $200 billion. In 1990, the Swiss pharmaceutical firm Hoffmann-LaRoche spent $2.1 billion to buy 60% of the shares of Genentech, a leading U.S. biotechnology company. In addition, the European community is encouraging alliances in technology through organizations such as the European Strategic Program for Research and Development in Information Technology (ESPRIT), which reviews and funds collaborative projects. By 1990, more than 1,000 companies were participating in several programs organized by ESPRIT, and they were expected to invest tens of billions of dollars during the 1990s.

GM and IBM already have large, profitable operations in Europe, and both have recently created alliances to strengthen their positions there. In late 1989, GM announced it would form a joint venture with Saab-Scania of Sweden by paying $600 million for a 50% stake in Saab's auto division. This product link gave GM immediate access to a line of sports and luxury sedans that it needed for the growing luxury car market in Europe and the United States. The two companies also planned a knowledge link: a joint venture in automotive electronics.[3] IBM's alliances in Europe, as in Japan and the United States, are smaller-scale ventures with a variety of firms, including specialized hardware and software makers. Other links involve national postal and telecommunications agencies, as well as companies that want to design and build "intelligent buildings," structures that use computers and telecommunications intensively. Analysts believed IBM's collaboration with Siemens would help it build relationships with European semiconductor consortia such as the Joint European Submicron Silicon Project (JESSI), in which Siemens, Philips, SGS-Thomson, and their governments were planning to invest $500 million a year.[4]

The historic changes in Eastern Europe also promise to accelerate the migration of knowledge. A large pool of educated, low-cost labor is opening up, immediately adjacent to the developed European economies. In the future, it promises large markets with enormous pent-up demand, as signified by the 10-year waiting lists for low-quality Eastern European cars. Japanese interest in these opportunities is awakening. At the end of 1989, for example, Suzuki Motor announced that it would create a joint venture in Hungary to build minicars. Suzuki's partners were C. Itoh, the giant Japanese trading company, a Hungarian holding company, Autokonszern, and the International Finance Corp., a World Bank affiliate. Through the deal, Suzuki gained entry to the Eastern European market as well as an export base for Eastern Europe. By mid-1990, GM had moved into Eastern Europe more rapidly than any other non-European firm. It announced a joint venture with Raba, a state-owned Hungarian truck maker, to produce cars and engines, and a joint venture with an East German auto company. GM was also holding talks with officials in Czechoslovakia, Poland, Hungary, and the Soviet Union about further steps in its "East Bloc Strategy."[5]

These highly publicized developments were part of much larger and more complex trends, which promised to accelerate the movement of knowledge across the boundaries of nations and companies. In early 1990, the Soviet Academy of Sciences and Arthur D. Little, the U.S.-based technology consulting firm, announced that they would jointly create a company, based in Geneva and Moscow, to develop Soviet science and technology and then commercialize it in the West. More than 30 Soviet research institutes were expected to participate, and the chairman of the Soviet Academy called the venture "a further step to internationalize the conduct of scientific research and the development of its applications."[6] By 1990, South Korea had helped create computer networks linking Hungarian and Polish firms with South Korean firms. South Korean firms were also negotiating for joint ventures in electronics, auto components, and other businesses in Eastern Europe, in part, perhaps, to open doors to the Soviet Union, where Japanese firms already had extensive contacts.[7] The number of registered joint ventures in the U.S.S.R. had risen from 200 in 1988 to over 1,000 in 1989, and roughly 100 had begun operations.

Uncertainties, of course, cloud the economic future of Europe. Pessimistic scenarios must be taken seriously but should not overwhelm analysis. After all, U.S. Secretary of State John Foster Dulles reportedly observed after World War II that "suicide is not an illogical step for anyone concerned about Japan's economic future."[8]

If optimistic scenarios prove accurate, the globalization of knowledge will continue. Firms and other organizations in Europe will contribute even more to the worldwide pool of commercializable knowledge. In response, product links and knowledge links will continue to knit together American, Japanese, and European companies. Competition will intensify, more alliances will be formed, and the boundaries of firms will grow even more complex. Perhaps the only answer to the question of what the future holds is this: if knowledge-based competition continues to intensify, many familiar ways of thinking and managing will change.

As before, a comparison with the Italian city-states is provocative and illuminating. The arts, letters, commerce, and technology flourished in Renaissance Italy amid uncertainty, turbulence, and sometimes violence and change. Civil and economic life unfolded within the interstices of elaborate, shifting alliances among the city-states and their rulers. The Renaissance brought relentless questioning and universal reexamination of ideas and practices rendered familiar and powerful by centuries of custom. The historian J.H. Plumb wrote of the period that:

> Sensitive, thoughtful men realized that
> this was a world like unto none other. . . . What
> made men succeed? or fail? Why did some cities
> grow rich only to dissipate it all in war and rebellion?

Why did free citizens become the prey of professional thugs? What were the causes of tyranny? Was
tyranny bad? Did cities have a natural life like
men—youth, maturity, age? And were learning, art,
and the practice of humanism bound up with the nature of citizens?[9]

      The blurring of firms' boundaries poses many ques-
tions for managers and scholars. Are other familiar boundaries,
for example, now eroding? Already, departments and functional
areas in many companies are no longer separate baronies. As
Peter Drucker has observed, "In pharmaceuticals, in telecommunications, in papermaking, the traditional *sequence* of research, development, manufacturing, and marketing is being
replaced by *synchrony*: specialists from all these functions work
together as a team, from the inception of research to a product's
establishment in the market."[10] Advances in computer technology and telecommunications have enabled companies to pare
away layers of middle management, reducing the barriers between
executives and company operations. For global companies that
run sourcing, assembly, logistics, inventories, finance, and marketing as an integrated worldwide system, traditional systems
based on separate, fairly independent national managers are cumbersome anachronisms.

      If boundaries between traditional departments blur
at the same time the boundaries of firms are blurring, will companies become less like hierarchies and more like networks? Will
the traditional vertical lines of authority from boss to subordinate
give way to horizontal relationships? A cluster of overlapping circles may come to represent a company more accurately than a
table of organization with a boss at the top. The center of the
cluster would represent a firm's core capabilities: knowledge and
skills embedded in complex relationships, including administrative, social, and contractual relationships. The surrounding circles would represent supporting skills, some owned and controlled
by the firm and others managed through knowledge links. Further

from the core would be the product links that supplement a company's product line, range of services, or supply of components.

How will managers' tasks change in response to these developments? The success of senior executives will probably come to depend more heavily on their ability to safeguard and strengthen their firms' core skills, in addition to their traditional responsibility of using those skills to produce competitive products. This task could be difficult, since companies will become even more decentralized than they already are, and the authority of managers will be dispersed across company boundaries. If a company creates knowledge links with its suppliers, its purchasing department will grow in size and expertise. It may also become a coordinating mechanism for relationships between engineers and marketing personnel inside the company and their counterparts in outside supplier firms. The department and its boss will fade away, replaced by complex knowledge links managed by teams of leaders. Finding ways to keep these diffuse teams focused and efficient—and defining new models of leadership for them—will be major challenges.

The future also holds new questions for government officials. Should antitrust policy encourage or discourage boundary-blurring activities among competitors? During the 1980s, U.S. officials were more tolerant of such tie-ups, but the GM-Toyota joint venture was approved only by a close vote, after intense scrutiny, and with lengthy and detailed restrictions on the collaboration. Generally, the government assesses each proposed joint effort to determine how the benefits to consumers compare with the harm caused by reduced competition. But if a growing number of companies propose cooperative endeavors, the government's limited resources for reviewing proposals may lead to delays and impair the competitiveness of U.S. companies.

Issues of social accountability are likely to grow even murkier. If a firm is a citadel, its executives can be held accountable for compliance with laws and regulations. But in a network of shared authority, where, in Harry Truman's phrase, does the buck stop? Moreover, if firms are not separate spheres of managerial control but economic, political, and social complexes linked to many other bodies in society, their political power may increase, and they may claim more persuasively to represent the broader interests of society and not just their shareholders' financial interests. What is good for General Motors, it will be argued anew, is good for the country.

All these possibilities and questions raise a final, broad, historical issue: perhaps firms that blur their boundaries are not creating a wholly new corporate form but rather recreating old patterns of doing business on a global scale. The history of commerce, until the Industrial Revolution, is essentially a chronicle of indefinite and permeable boundaries around business activities. "Business" was enmeshed in relationships with families, because households were basic economic units; with villages and manors, the organizing units of agriculture; with guilds, which regulated the relations of master, journeymen, and apprentices; and with towns and their customs, which shaped and regulated the behavior of guilds and their workers. Only in Great Britain, about 200 years ago, did a self-regulating market of separate economic units appear. But even there, the market capitalism of independent competing firms did not spring full-blown into existence. Rather, separate economic units emerged only slowly from the social and political webs that had enveloped them for so long.[11] When Britain's rapid industrialization and growing economic might frightened the French, Prussian, and later the German governments, they responded by promoting and directing economic activity through subsidies, state ownership, cartels, protection, and administrative guidance—all of which obscured the boundaries among firms and between states and firms. After Admiral Perry's "barbarians" had humbled the proud nation, Japan created many similar arrangements.

Against the broad sweep of the history of commerce and business organization, companies as citadels—clearly defined zones of ownership and control surrounded by market relations— are the anomaly. This form of economic organization will not disappear, but it is changing dramatically, in ways that could again reshape economic life. That may be the larger picture emerging from the intricate mosaic of today's strategic alliances.

Notes

Introduction

1. Thinking of a firm as a citadel or a stronghold is a doubly powerful metaphor, for castles were also symbols. The English, for example, continued to build castles after the fourteenth century, even though they had become military anachronisms, because they represented strength, permanence, prestige, security, and authority. As symbols, they drew together many diverse strands of medieval life. See, for example, W. Douglas Simpson, *Castles in England and Wales* (Aberdeen, Scotland: Aberdeen University Press, 1969), pp. 1–15; Plantagenet Somerset Fry, *British Medieval Castles* (London: David & Charles, 1974), pp. 1–23.

2. Max Weber described the basic mechanisms of hierarchical control in his conceptualization of the "ideal type" of rational bureaucratic management. Specialization, roles assigned by technical competence, or hierarchy of authority, standard operating procedures, and clear specification of responsibility all marked off the individuals and activities inside an organization. The company stopped where the formal, hierarchical structures stopped. Others, such as Chester Barnard, acknowledged that firms' boundaries were more open and fluid, but Barnard himself argued that firms had a "periphery" at which they and other organizations exchanged goods and funds. See Chester I. Barnard, *The Functions of the Executive* (Cambridge, MA: Harvard University Press, 1968), pp. 138–160.

   Berle and Means' classic analysis suggests another way in which firms' administrative boundaries were sharpened. In essence, owners ceded control over the operations of companies to full-time managers in return for liquidity and assured returns on their investments. Two separate groups were created out of what had been a single group, "the owners without appreciable control and the control without appreciable ownership." See Adolf A. Berle and Gardiner C. Means, *The Modern Corporation as Private Property* (New York: Macmillan Company, 1933), p. 121.

3. A recent study concluded that the best way to describe the financial strategies of American firms was as a pursuit of "self-sufficiency." That is, "managements rely heavily on retained earnings to meet the demand for funds from their

existing businesses. Retained earnings are particularly appropriate for this purpose because they are the source about which management has the best information and over which *it has the greatest control*" (emphasis added). See Gordon
Donaldson, *Managing Corporate Wealth* (New York: Praeger, 1984), p. 46.
Another study, which examined the equity financing of 250 of the *Fortune* 500
companies between 1940 and 1978, found that only one in five had sold
common stock for internal purposes (as opposed to selling stock when they
initially went public or to finance an acquisition) and fewer than one in ten
had sold equity more than once during this 38-year period. See Richard R.
Ellsworth, "Subordinate Financial Policy to Corporate Strategy," *Harvard Business Review* (November–December 1983), p. 171. Similar findings, based on
more recent data, appear in Krishna G. Palepu and Paul M. Healy, "How
Investors Interpret Changes in Corporate Financial Policy," *Continental Bank
Journal of Applied Corporate Finance* (Fall 1989), pp. 59–64.
4. Robert Nozick, *Anarchy, State, and Utopia* (New York: Basic Books, 1974),
p. 163.
5. The conception of a firm as a social body originated in the writings of the
sociologist Ferdinand Tonnies. His ideas matured in the same era in which
Weber came to view firms as systems defined, in large measure, by hierarchical
controls and in which the classical economists defined firms as spheres of
managerial discretion. The notion of a firm as a citadel melds Tonnies's insights
with those of Weber and the economists. Tonnies distinguished two fundamentally different social entities. One he called a *Gesellschaft*, a group that is
formed intentionally to achieve a specific objective. Its value depends on how
well it does so. The other kind of group, a *Gemeinschaft*, arises unintentionally
from habit, mutual sympathy, or common beliefs, and it is valued as an end
in itself. Neighborhoods, religious bodies, and towns are examples of the *Gemeinschaft*. See Ferdinand Tonnies, *Community and Society* (East Lansing,
MI: Michigan State University Press, 1957), pp. 16–28. Tonnies's ideas were
applied to modern public and private organizations in Philip Selznick, *Leadership in Administration* (New York: Harper & Row, 1957), in particular,
pp. 17 and 93–94. Another variation on Tonnies's basic theme was developed
by James MacGregor Burns when he distinguished "transcending" leadership
from "transactional" leadership; see James MacGregor Burns, *Leadership* (New
York: Harper & Row, 1978), pp. 1–32.
      More recently, a Japanese scholar has described his nation's firms
as "capsules" to emphasize that they were closed societies providing their members with security, friendships, and opportunities for self-realization and contributions to society. The relationship between these firms and their members
involves "a dependence of the whole personality" of the employee or manager.
The firm was their "cozy shelter, so arranged that when the chilly wind rages
outside, one can enjoy a comfortable life inside." See Moriaki Tsuchiya, "The
Japanese Business as a *Capsule*," *Japanese Economic Studies* 8 (Fall 1989),
pp. 8–41.

6. This account of classical contracting is based upon Ian R. MacNeil, "Contracts: Adjustment of Long-term Economic Relations under Classical, Neoclassical, and Relational Contract Law," *Northwestern University Law Review* 72 (June 1978), pp. 854–905; and Ian R. MacNeil, "The Many Futures of Contracts," *Southern California Law Review* 47 (May 1974), pp. 691–816.

7. Chapter 4 offers a detailed conceptualization of companies as social devices for creating, storing, processing, and transmitting information.

8. Hiroyuki Itami, *Mobilizing Invisible Assets* (Cambridge, MA: Harvard University Press, 1987), p. 30.

9. Of course, managers were often ambivalent about collaborative practices, favoring vigorous competition as a general principle, fearing collusion by their competitors, but open to cartels and other forms of cooperation from which they would benefit.

10. Daniel Katz and Robert L. Kahn, *The Social Psychology of Organizations* (New York: John Wiley, 1966), p. 122.

11. Michael C. Jensen and William H. Meckling, "The Theory of the Firm: Managerial Behavior, Agency Costs, and Ownership Structure," *Journal of Financial Economics* (Fall 1976), p. 311.

12. Robert Eccles, "The Quasifirm in the Construction Industry," *Journal of Economic Behavior and Organization* (December 1981), pp. 335–357.

13. Dennis H. Robertson, *Control of Industry* (London: Nisbet and Co., 1930), p. 85.

14. Most studies of the incidence of cooperative arrangements reach this conclusion. One exception is a study of "international coalitions"—defined as "joint ventures, licenses, supply agreements, and other long-term firm accords"— reported in *The Wall Street Journal* between 1970 and 1982. It found no clear increase or decrease in coalition activity during this period. See Pankaj Ghemawat, Michael E. Porter, and Richard A. Rawlinson, "Patterns of International Coalition Activity," in *Competition in Global Industries*, Michael E. Porter, ed. (Boston: Harvard Business School Press, 1986), pp. 345–365. Research by Benjamin Gomes-Casseres, focusing on joint ventures between multinational firms and local partners between World War II and 1975, suggests that the incidence of joint ventures may follow a cyclical pattern. See Benjamin Gomes-Casseres, "Multinational Ownership Strategies," unpublished Ph.D. diss., Harvard Business School, 1985, pp. 405–459.

15. Kathryn Rudie Harrigan, *Strategies for Joint Ventures* (Lexington, MA: D. C. Heath, 1985), pp. 7–12.

16. Karen J. Hladik, "International Joint Ventures," Ph.D. diss., Harvard Business School, 1984, p. 56.

17. Ibid., p. 64.

18. Norm Alster, "Electronics Firms Find Strength in Numbers," *Electronic Business* 12, no. 5 (March 1, 1986), pp. 102–104, 106, 108.

19. Martin Kenney, *Biotechnology: The University-Industrial Complex* (New Haven: Yale University Press, 1987).

20. See, for example, William C. Freund and Eugene Epstein, *People and Productivity* (Homewood, IL: Dow Jones-Irwin, 1984), pp. 128–129; Y. K. Shetty and Vernon M. Buehler, eds., *Productivity and Quality through People* (Westport, CT: Quorum Books, 1985); Roger W. Bergerand and David L. Shores, eds., *Quality Circles* (New York: Marcel Dekker, 1986); Richard B. Kopelman, *Managing Productivity in Organizations* (New York: McGraw-Hill, 1986).

21. For an overview of recent trends toward activist shareholders, see Michael C. Jensen, "The Eclipse of the Public Corporation," *Harvard Business Review* (September–October 1989), pp. 61–74.

22. The academic literature on joint ventures and other collaborative arrangements provides many ways of categorizing these relationships. A common approach uses a spectrum of ownership and legal arrangements ranging from technical assistance and licensing, at one end, to original equipment manufacturing (OEM) deals, through joint development, joint standard setting, joint ventures and consortia, and ultimately to 100% direct investments, at the other end of the spectrum. See, for example, Louis Turner, *Industrial Collaboration with Japan* (London: Routledge & Kegan Paul, 1987), pp. 5–10. Others have made even finer distinctions among various types of collaboration. For example, joint ventures may be distinguished by the motives that led to their creation. One study lists fourteen separate subcategories. See Harrigan, *Strategies for Joint Ventures*, p. 18.

It is also possible to look at relations between firms and other organizations and distinguish formal and informal links, bilateral and multilateral links, partnerships with competitors and noncompetitors, formal and informal contracts, and so forth. The reason these categories and subcategories have grown so complex is that they attempt to sort out the motives, forms, activities, and participants in the almost wildly heterogeneous realm of relationships that have linked firms and other organizations, whether recently or in the distant past.

23. Personal correspondence with Tadashi Okamura, External Relations, IBM Japan, April 8, 1988.

24. Herbert A. Simon, "The Impact of the Computer on Management," presented at the 15th CIOS World Conference, Tokyo, 1969, cited in Yoneji Masuda, *The Information Society* (Tokyo: Institute for the Information Society, 1980), p. xv.

25. An argument that cartels can and often do serve valuable economic and social ends is made in Joseph L. Bower and Eric A. Rhenman, "Benevolent Cartels," *Harvard Business Review* (July–August 1985), pp. 124–132.

26. See Alfred D. Chandler, Jr., *Strategy and Structure: Chapters in the History of American Industrial Enterprise* (Cambridge, MA: MIT Press, 1962), p. 14.

27. This question is arguably the central concern of a rapidly growing body of concepts and research called the "new institutional economics." The initial concern of scholars doing this work was the question of why economic activity

is sometimes organized (or "governed") by firms and sometimes by markets. More recently, the problem has been posed in a more complex and more realistic way: scholars have asked why these governance structures are sometimes firms, sometimes markets, and sometimes "hybrid" arrangements, like those examined in this study. For an encompassing overview of these concepts and their evolution, see Oliver E. Williamson, *The Economic Institutions of Capitalism* (New York: Free Press, 1985), pp. 1–84.

28. This generalization is not meant as a universal rule. Sears, for example, has cooperated with some of its many suppliers in developing products.

29. This metaphor, like any other, makes only a partial comparison. The differences between firms and city-states include the intertwining, in the latter, of family loyalties and rivalries with affairs of state; the predatory, manipulative, often violent behavior of the Borgias of Milan and the leaders of other city-states; and the enormous size of many companies, which makes them similar to nation-states.

30. Hiroyuki Itami has conceptualized this knowledge, as well as a firm's manufacturing and marketing know-how and its customers' image of a company, as "invisible assets." Itami, *Mobilizing Invisible Assets*, pp. 27–30, 53–54.

Chapter 1

1. A list of many of these transformations and their sources appears in James R. Beniger, *The Control Revolution* (Cambridge, MA: Harvard University Press, 1986), pp. 4–5.

2. John Stuart Mill, *Principles of Political Economy* (London: Longmans, Green, Reeder, and Dyer, 1871), p. 422.

3. In many contexts, the term "global" is an overstatement. Typically, the "global market" is actually a regional market, usually in developed countries, and only a handful of products—the Sony Walkman, the Volkswagen Beetle, some U.S. cigarette brands, for example—have been successfully marketed on a worldwide basis. For a detailed analysis of the many facets of globalization, see Michael E. Porter, ed., *Competition in Global Industries* (Boston: Harvard Business School Press, 1986).

4. For further discussion, see Robert E. Everson, "International Invention: Implications for Technology Market Analysis," in *R&D, Patents, and Productivity*, Zvi Griliches, ed. (Chicago: University of Chicago Press, 1984), pp. 89–123; and Frederic M. Scherer, "Comment," Ibid., pp. 123–124.

5. Kenneth Boulding, "The Knowledge Explosion," in *To Nurture Humaneness: Commitments for the 1970s*, Mary-Margaret Scobey and Grace Graham, eds. (Washington, DC: National Educational Association, 1970), p. 88.

6. The different categories of knowledge and the quotation are taken from Fritz Machlup, *The Production and Distribution of Knowledge in the United States* (Princeton, NJ: Princeton University Press, 1962), pp. 13–22. A broad overview

of the peculiar characteristics of knowledge as a good is Daniel Bell, *The Coming of Post-Industrial Society* (New York: Basic Books, 1976), pp. xii–xvi. The economics of information are analyzed in Kenneth J. Arrow, *Information and Economic Behavior* (Stockholm: Svanback & Nymans Boctryckeri, 1973), pp. 5–28.

7. Kenneth Boulding, "The Economics of Knowledge and the Knowledge of Economics," *American Economic Review* (May 1966), p. 1.

8. Bell, *The Coming of Post-Industrial Society*, p. 174.

9. Peter F. Drucker, *The Age of Discontinuity* (New York: Harper & Row, 1968), p. 263.

10. Stanley R. Rich and David E. Gumpert, "What's New in the Superconductivity Business," *New York Times*, January 24, 1988, p. F17.

11. This broad definition gathers together as "knowledge" many phenomena that, for different purposes, scholars and analysts have distinguished. Historians of technology have, for example, debated whether technology should be regarded as its own sphere of knowledge or whether it is fundamentally the applied form of the "genuine" knowledge created by scientists. For a review of these issues, see Edwin T. Layton, Jr., "Technology as Knowledge," *Technology and Culture* (January 1974), pp. 31–41. Chapter 5 discusses this particular issue at length.

12. Thomas S. Eliot, "Choruses from 'The Rock,' " *Collected Poems, 1909–1962* (New York: Harcourt, Brace & World, 1965), p. 147.

13. David S. Landes, *The Unbound Prometheus* (Cambridge: Cambridge University Press, 1969), p. 98.

14. Benniger, *The Control Revolution*, p. 7. Benniger traces the history of devices and methods for controlling information even further back into history, and he stresses the acceleration in the development of these technologies resulting from, first, the Industrial Revolution, next, the rise of giant enterprises at the end of the nineteenth century, and only then, the availability of computer hardware and software in the past 25 years.

15. The data underlying this approximation are presented and analyzed in Derek de Solla Price, *Science Since Babylon* (New Haven: Yale University Press, 1975), pp. 161–179.

16. Ibid., p. 164.

17. Kimio Uno, "Recent Trends in R&D and Patents," in *R&D Management Systems in Japanese Industry*, Hajime Eto and Konomu Matsui, eds. (Amsterdam: North Holland, 1984), pp. 121–123; and David M. Levy and Nestor E. Terleckyj, *Trends in Industrial R&D Activities in the United States, Europe, and Japan, 1963–1983*, unpublished paper presented at the National Bureau of Economic Research Conference on Productivity Growth in Japan and the United States, August 1985, Cambridge, MA.

18. Bell, *The Coming of Post-Industrial Society*, p. 187.

19. See Fumio Kodama, "Alternative Innovation: Innovation through Technological Fusion," *Science*, July 18, 1986, pp. 291–296.

20. "A Sputtering Start," *The Economist*, April 30, 1988, p. 84; and Dennis Kneale, "Superconducting 'Thin Films' Tests IBM's Talent, Patience," *The Wall Street Journal*, September 11, 1987, p. 29.
21. Dietrich Altenpohl, *Materials in World Perspective* (Berlin: Springer-Verlag, 1980), pp. 120–122.
22. The examples are drawn from David Stipp, "Scientists Seeking to Put Life Into Body Replacement Parts," *The Wall Street Journal*, September 25, 1987, p. 29; and David Stipp, "High-Speed Photography Sheds Image as a Tricky Craft with Few Applications," *The Wall Street Journal*, July 1, 1988, p. 19. An overview of the role of scientific technique in increasing scientific knowledge is Frederick Betz, *Managing Technology* (Englewood Cliffs, NJ: Prentice-Hall, 1987), pp. 231–242.
23. H. M. Chang, J. J. Day, and W. S. Lee, "Chinese Information on Medicinal Materials Computerization Project," in *Towards the Information Society*, Ramon C. Barquin and Graham P. Mead, eds. (Amsterdam: North Holland, 1984), pp. 141–149.
24. These examples are taken from Yoneji Masuda, *The Information Society* (Tokyo: Institute for the Information Society, 1980), pp. 42–44; and Michael J. C. Martin, *Managing Technological Innovation and Entrepreneurship* (Reston, VA: Reston Publishing Company, 1984), pp. 19–23.
25. D. Bruce Merrifield, "Forces of Change Affecting High Technology Industries," *National Journal*, January 29, 1983, p. 255.
26. Johannes Hirschmeyer and T. Yui, *The Development of Japanese Business, 1969–1973* (Cambridge, MA: Harvard University Press, 1975), p. 258.
27. Sector-by-sector trends for research-intensive products are presented and analyzed in Bruce R. Scott, "National Strategies: Key to International Competition," in *U.S. Competitiveness in the World Economy*, Bruce R. Scott and George C. Lodge, eds. (Boston: Harvard Business School Press, 1985), pp. 71–144. See the series of "Competitive Assessments," published by the U.S. Department of Commerce between 1985 and 1987. They analyze the U.S. competitive position in more than 50 industries.
28. "Into the Mind Field," *The Economist*, January 30, 1988, p. 68.
29. Joel Dreyfuss, "How Japan Picks America's Brains," *Fortune*, December 21, 1987, p. 88.
30. Otis Port, "Cash-rich Japan and a Unifying Europe Are Closing the Gap in Science," *BusinessWeek*, June 15, 1990, p. 36.
31. De Solla Price, *Science Since Babylon*, p. 181.

Chapter 2

1. Jonathan Clements, "Money-Manager Math Whiz Calls It Quits," *The Wall Street Journal*, February 11, 1990, p. B1.
2. See Hitachi Annual Reports, 1982 to 1985; David B. Tinnin, " 'Jap Scam' for Computer Spies," *Fortune*, July 26, 1982, p. 7, and "How IBM Stung

Hitachi," *Fortune*, March 7, 1983, pp. 50–56; and Robert Sobel, *IBM vs. Japan* (New York: Stein & Day, 1986), pp. 167–171.

3. Richard R. Nelson and Sidney G. Winter, *An Evolutionary Theory of Economic Change* (Cambridge, MA: Harvard University Press, 1982), p. 60.

4. Kenneth Boulding, "The Economics of Knowledge and the Knowledge of Economics," *American Economic Review* (May 1966), p. 4.

5. Edwin Mansfield, "R&D and Innovation," in R&D, *Patents and Productivity*, Zvi Griliches, ed. (Chicago: University of Chicago Press, 1984), pp. 142–143.

6. Ennius Bergsma, "Do-It-Yourself Takeover Curbs," *The Wall Street Journal*, February 12, 1988, p. 26.

7. David S. Landes, *The Unbound Prometheus* (Cambridge: Cambridge University Press, 1969), pp. 61–64.

8. Franklin M. Fisher, James W. McKie, and Richard B. Mancke, *IBM and the U.S. Data-Processing Industry: An Economic History* (New York: Praeger, 1983), p. 416.

9. James P. Miller, "Amdahl Unveiled a Faster Line of Computers," *The Wall Street Journal*, May 4, 1988, p. 4.

10. Charles H. Ferguson, "Sources and Implications of Strategic Decline: The Case of Japanese-American Competition in Microelectronics," Massachusetts Institute of Technology, unpublished paper, June 30, 1987, p. 10.

11. Andrew Grove, "The Future of Silicon Valley," *California Management Review*, vol. 29, no. 3 (Spring 1987), pp. 156–157.

12. "Alien Academics," *The Wall Street Journal*, October 24, 1985, p. 35.

13. Everett Rogers's work is an example of the latter. In fact, the study of the diffusion of innovation is itself an example of the accelerating growth of knowledge, its migration, and its creation in an ever-widening range of countries. An early classic is *The Diffusion of Innovations*, by Everett M. Rogers, first published in 1962, when there were 405 publications available on the subject. When the second edition appeared in 1971, the number had quadrupled to approximately 1,400. When the most recent edition was published in 1983, the number had doubled to more than 3,000. Rogers observed, "I think there is almost no other field of behavioral science research that represents more effort by more scholars in more nations."

      Rogers's work is a macrotheoretical effort. He argues that five factors synthesize the efforts of social scientists to account for the diffusion of a vast range of innovations—family planning techniques, high technology, clothing fashions, the practice of boiling drinking water, and political philosophies and ideologies—and account for the pace at which innovations are adopted. These are the *relative advantage* of the innovation over the idea it supersedes; its *compatibility* with the values and past experiences of potential adopters; its *complexity*, which determines how difficult it is to understand and use; its *trialability*, or the degree to which it may be experimented with on a limited basis; and its *observability*, or the degree to which its results can be seen by others. Everett M. Rogers, *The Diffusion of Innovations* (New York: Free Press, 1983), p. xv.

14. Nathan Rosenberg, *Perspectives on Technology* (Cambridge: Cambridge University Press, 1976). These quotations appear on pp. 28, 83.

15. The concept of complementary assets has been developed by David J. Teece, "Profiting from Technological Innovation: Implications for Integration, Collaboration, Licensing and Public Policy," *Research Policy*, November 15, 1986, pp. 285–305.

16. Michael A. Cusumano, *The Japanese Automobile Industry* (Cambridge, MA: Council on East Asian Studies, Harvard University, 1985), p. 65.

17. The phrase "invisible colleges" first appeared in Derek J. de Solla Price, *Little Science Big Science* (New York: Columbia University Press, 1963), p. 73.

18. Keith Pavitt, "Technology Transfer Among the Industrially Advanced Countries," in *International Technology Transfer*, Nathan Rosenberg and Claudio Frischtak, eds. (New York: Praeger, 1985), p. 4.

19. Alfred Marshall, *Principles of Economics* (New York: Macmillan Company, 1920), p. 285.

20. The original statement of the product life cycle theory of trade is Raymond Vernon's in "International Investment and International Trade in the Product Cycle," *Quarterly Journal of Economics*, vol. 80 (May 1966), pp. 109–207. An overview is found in *The Product Life Cycle and International Trade*, Louis T. Wells, Jr., ed. (Boston: Division of Research, Harvard Business School, 1972.)

21. Mansfield, "R&D and Innovation," pp. 138–139.

22. See Robert Stobaugh, "Channels for Technology Transfer: The Petrochemical Industry," in *Technology Crossing Borders*, Louis T. Wells, Jr., and Robert Stobaugh, eds. (Boston: Harvard Business School Press, 1984), pp. 157–176.

23. Norman Gall, "Does Anyone Really Believe in Free Trade?," *Forbes*, December 14, 1986, p. 119.

24. A thorough, succinct overview of the economic rationale for commercial secrecy, including its treatment in the law and economics literature is Kim Lane Scheppele, *Legal Secrets* (Chicago: University of Chicago Press, 1988), pp. 24–42. See Richard R. Nelson, "The Simple Economics of Basic Scientific Research," *Journal of Political Economy*, vol. 67, pp. 297–306; Kenneth J. Arrow, *Essays in the Theory of Risk-Bearing* (Amsterdam: North-Holland, 1971), Chapter 6, for statements on the basic problem of appropriating the profits from innovation.

"Appropriability" is now used as an explanatory variable in econometric models intended to explain how firms and industries invest in R&D. See, for example, Ariel Pakes and Mark Schankerman, "The Rate of Obsolescence of Patents, Research, Gestation Lags, and the Private Rate of Return to Research Resources," in *R&D, Patents, and Productivity*, Griliches, ed., pp. 73–88. David Teece has applied the concept of "regimes of appropriability" to international firms' decisions about investment and organization. Under "tight appropriability," the legal system protects the rights of owners of intellectual property; under "loose appropriability," it does so only partially. See David J. Teece, "The Market for Know-How and the Efficient International Transfer of Technology," *Annals of the American Academy of Political and Social Science*, November 1981, pp. 81–96; and Teece, "Profiting from Technological Innovation," pp. 285–305.

25. Lawrence Ingrassia and Clare Ansberry, "Polaroid Seeks Patent Damages of $5.7 Billion," *The Wall Street Journal*, February 22, 1988, p. 2.

26. See "Biotechnology," *The Economist*, April 30, 1988, p. 18; *Intellectual Property Rights in an Age of Electronics and Information* (Washington, DC: U.S. Office of Technology Assessment, 1986), p. 300; H. Stalson, *Intellectual Property Rights and U.S. Competitiveness in Trade* (Washington, DC: National Planning Association, 1987); Miles R. Gilburne, *Intellectual Property Rights in High-Technology Products and in Sensitive Business Information* (New York: Harcourt, 1982); United States House of Representatives, *Unfair Foreign Trade Practices: Stealing American Intellectual Property: Imitation Is Not Flattery* (Washington, DC, 1984), p. 65; and Jonathan P. Levine, "Cutting the Heart Out of European Biotech?," *BusinessWeek*, June 18, 1990, pp. 177–178.

27. Everett M. Rogers and Judith K. Rogers, *Silicon Valley Fever* (New York: Basic Books, 1984), p. 64.

28. This description of the evolution of the personal computer business is drawn from Paul Freiberger and Michael Swaine, *Fire in the Valley* (Berkeley, CA: Osborne/McGraw-Hill, 1984); Geoff Lewis, "The PC Wars: IBM versus the Clones," *BusinessWeek*, July 28, 1986, pp. 62–68; Patricia B. Graw, "Asian Computer Firms Invade the U.S. Market for Personal Machines," *The Wall Street Journal*, January 10, 1986, p. 1; William Zachmann, "As 1990 Nears, IBM Faces Change and Challenge," *Computer World*, December 3, 1986, pp. 2–6; Paul B. Carroll and Hank Gilman, "Mainframe Slowdown and Stiff Competition Put Pressure on IBM," *The Wall Street Journal*, November 23, 1987, p. 1; Alan Alper, "Tandy Clones Target Big Firms," *Computer World*, August 4, 1986, p. 1; news release from Cordata Technologies, November 2, 1987; "Who Will Copy the Kopy-Kats?," *The Economist*, November 15, 1986, p. 80.

29. Freiberger and Swaine, *Fire in the Valley*, pp. 276–277.

30. John B. Rae, *The American Automobile Industry* (Boston: G. K. Hall, 1984), pp. 11–13.

31. This account of the growth of the Japanese automobile industry is drawn from Cusumano, *The Japanese Automobile Industry*, Chapters 1, 2.

32. This account of the development of the South Korean automobile industry is based on Thomas Lowry, *The South Korean Motor Industry: A Re-Run of Japan?* (London: *The Economist*, 1987); Jung-nam Chi, "Economic Report: South Korea," *Asian Business*, vol. 22 (May 1986), pp. 37–56; Kevin Mos-

kowitz, *From Patron to Partner: The Development of U.S.-Korean Business and Trade Relations* (Lexington, MA: Lexington Books, 1985); International Bank for Reconstruction and Development, *Korea: Development in a Global Context* (Washington, DC: World Bank, 1984); and Tony Moyer, *The Korean Auto Industry* (Seoul: W.I. Carr, 1986).

Chapter 3

1. Joseph A. Schumpeter, *Capitalism, Socialism and Democracy* (New York: Harper & Row, 1975), p. 84.
2. See "Nissan Motor Group to Link with GM," *Nihon Keizai Shimbun*, December 16, 1985, p. 1; "Nissan Motor Group to Tie Up with GM in Auto Parts Production," *Nihon Keizai Shimbun*, December 28, 1985, p. 4; "NHK Spring to Undertake Joint Production with GM in U.S.," *Jiji Press Service*, April 25, 1986, p. 1, and "New Strategy of Auto Parts Makers," *Nihon Keizai Shimbun*, January 18, 1986, p. 10; "GM, Akebono to Set Up Brake Venture in U.S.," *Japan Economic Journal*, August 13, 1985, p. 1.
3. This account of IBM Japan's small computer efforts is based on interviews with IBM Japan executives, April 1988; internal documents provided by IBM Japan; Noaki Fukuzaki, "IBM Starts Full-Scale Offensive to Cut into OA Equipment Market," *Japan Economic Journal*, April 19, 1983, p. 5; "IBM Japan Limited," case material of the Nomura School of Advanced Management, Tokyo, 1984, pp. 33–38; "Matsushita to Double Supply of 16-bit PCs to IBM Japan," *Japan Economic Journal*, August 27, 1987, p. 11; "IBM Japan's PC Sales Are Reportedly Booming," *MIS Week*, August 28, 1985, p. 27; "ComputerLand Forms Japan Joint Venture," *The Wall Street Journal*, June 17, 1982, p. 16; Minoru Inaba, "IBM Japan Adds 8086-Based Matsushita-made Kanji PC," *Electronic News*, March 21, 1983, p. 24; Peter E. McKie, "Seeing Beyond PC Boundaries," *Personal Computing*, June 1987, pp. 110–115; "IBM Japan NS & I System Service Corporation to be Established," press release, IBM Japan, January 28, 1988; and Masayoshi Kanabayashi, "Nippon Steel, IBM Plan Joint Venture to Sell Computers," *The Wall Street Journal*, January 29, 1988, p. 6.
4. Maryann Keller, *Rude Awakening* (New York: William Morrow, 1989), p. 83.
5. Davis Dyer, Malcolm S. Salter, and Alan M. Webber, *Changing Alliances* (Boston: Harvard Business School Press, 1987), p. 152.
6. Personal interview with Suzuki executive, April 1987.
7. Yoshinori Fuiii, Suzuki Motor Company, quoted in William L. Veghte, "The Two Forces of Strategic Alliance: A Case Study of the Alliance Between Suzuki and General Motors," unpublished honors thesis, Harvard College, March 1990, p. 70.
8. Ibid., p. 73.
9. A detailed analysis of distribution-oriented alliances appears in Kenichi

Ohmae, "The Global Logic of Strategic Alliances," *Harvard Business Review* (March–April 1989), pp. 143–154.

10. This account of the GM-Daewoo relationship is based upon interviews with executives at GM, the Daewoo Motor Company, and the Daewoo Group as well as Melinda G. Guiles, "GM and Daewoo Plan Future Venture for Small Cars," *The Wall Street Journal*, June 15, 1984, p. 8; Douglas R. Sease, "South Korea Will Buy in U.S. Auto to Spur its Economy," *The Wall Street Journal*, September 16, 1984, p. 1; "Growing on Risk, Takeovers, and Innovation," *Business Korea* (June 1984), pp. 17–32; "Korean OK for GM," *Automotive News*, September 9, 1985, p. 1; "Korea Okays GM-Daewoo Ventures," *American Metal Market*, September 16, 1985, p. 5; Jacqueline Reditt, "What's Good for GM Is Not Necessarily Good for Korea," *The Far Eastern Economic Review*, February 27, 1981, p. 57; Mary Connelly, "LeMans Returns to Pontiac," *Automotive News*, February 6, 1986, p. 1; Andrew Tank, "Korea Launches New Wave of Exports to the U.S.," *Automotive News*, December 15, 1986, p. E-1.

11. GM's triumph is described in *My Years With General Motors* (Garden City, NY: Doubleday, 1963), and it is analyzed in Alfred D. Chandler, Jr., *Strategy and Structure: Chapters on the History of American Industrial Enterprise* (Cambridge, MA: MIT Press, 1962), pp. 114–162.

12. The authoritative history of IBM's computer business, covering the 1950s through the late 1970s, is Franklin M. Fisher, James W. McKie, and Richard B. Mancke, *IBM and the U.S. Data Processing Industry* (New York: Praeger, 1983). IBM's earlier history is presented in Saul Englebourg, *International Business Machines: A Business History* (New York: Arno Press, 1976); in Robert Sobel, *IBM: Colossus in Transition* (New York: Truman Talley, 1981); and in William Rogers, *Think: A Biography of the Watsons and IBM* (New York: Stein and Day, 1969).

Chapter 4

1. Sociologist Mark Granovetter has used the term "embeddedness" in an analogous fashion. In a frequently cited analysis, he contrasts various historical and contemporary views—from Thomas Hobbes and Adam Smith to Oliver Williamson and Talcott Parsons—on the degree to which economic behavior is embedded in social relationships or is independent of them. My focus is on the degree to which *knowledge* is embedded in such relations. See Mark Granovetter, "Economic Action and Social Structure: The Problem of Embeddedness," *American Journal of Sociology* (November 1985), pp. 481–510.

2. The power of our assumptions about individual knowledge is discussed in Mary Douglas, *How Institutions Think* (Syracuse: Syracuse University Press, 1986), pp. 9–19.

3. Michael Polanyi used the example of Stradivari to illustrate what he calls tacit knowledge. This is knowledge that cannot be made fully explicit, even by the person who has it. Near the end of his life, Polanyi sought to establish a new conception of all knowledge, including scientific knowledge, that rejected the common view that knowing something meant gaining a detached comprehension of an objective reality. At the same time, he did not believe that knowledge was wholly subjective. Rather, he argued that some knowledge was "personal," a "fusion of the personal and the objective," involving "passionate participation in the act of knowing." See Michael Polanyi, *Personal Knowledge* (Chicago: University of Chicago Press, 1948), pp. viii, 17. Polanyi's work has been called both obscurantist and seminal. A sympathetic overview of Polanyi's thinking is Richard Gelwick, *The Way of Discovery* (New York: Oxford University Press, 1977). The modern British philosopher, Gilbert Ryle, develops a similar distinction between "knowing that" and "knowing how" in his book *The Concept of Mind* (Chicago: University of Chicago Press, 1984), pp. 29–34. Another related concept is "background knowledge" as developed in Kim Lane Schleppele, *Legal Secrets* (Chicago: University of Chicago Press, 1987), pp. 25–26.

4. Alberto Bachmann, *An Encyclopedia of the Violin*, translated by Frederick H. Martens (New York: D. Appleton, 1925), p. 42.

5. In the words of one study:

> They had to be thoroughly familiar with the machinery with which they worked, its capabilities and limitations. The same was true of the materials they worked on. These machinists had to know the proper tools, speeds, and feeds for the various types of metal, and be able to change these variables quickly due to the variant and unreliable nature of the materials. And these skills were not theoretical, not formulated into a precise body of written rules and laws. They were largely empirical, gained mainly through long apprenticeship training and experience in watching and doing work itself. Machinists' skills were a series of a thousand little knacks. . . . workers learned intuitively to "feel" if the tool was getting dull, if the tool speed was too fast, if the casting was of poor quality.

See David Gartman, *Auto Slavery* (Rutgers, NJ: Rutgers University Press, 1986), p. 29. Similarly, Shoshana Zuboff distinguishes between embodied or action-centered skills from intellectual skills. See Shoshana Zuboff, *In the Age of the Smart Machine* (New York: Basic Books, 1988), pp. 70–79.

6. Richard R. Nelson and Sidney G. Winter, *An Evolutionary Theory of Economic Change* (Cambridge, MA: Harvard University Press, 1982), p. 62.

7. The basic characteristics of this sort of personal expertise and the cognitive

conditions underlying it are described in Michael J. Prietula and Herbert A. Simon, "The Experts in Your Midst," *Harvard Business Review* (January–February 1989), pp. 120–124.

8. Koji Kobayashi, *Computers and Communications* (Cambridge, MA: MIT Press, 1986), p. 85.

9. Of course, some skilled craftsmen do move from company to company and take their skills with them, but they can put these skills to work quickly only if they find the proper combination of technological, economic, and social arrangements in their new place of employment. Samuel Slater, the Englishman who founded the American cotton industry, left England in 1789, disguised as a farm boy to evade laws prohibiting the emigration of textile workers. When he arrived in Rhode Island, Slater could not go to work in the Richard A. Arkwright-designed mills he knew and helped manage in England as Arkwright's partner. No such mills existed. They had to be created, and Slater spent his early years in America doing so. In the language of Oliver Williamson, Slater's skills were *asset-specific*. He had to create assets (the mill) that complemented his own before he could put his skills to their full use. See Oliver Williamson, *The Economic Institutions of Capitalism* (New York: Free Press, 1985).

10. Frederick A. Hayek, "The Use of Knowledge in Society," *The American Economic Review* (September 1945), pp. 521–522.

11. Emile Durkheim first analyzed the many ways in which particular institutions and society as a whole provided categories, conventions of thought, collective attitudes, and guiding metaphors to individuals. An extended discussion of Durkheim's thinking on this issue, synthesized with more recent work in sociology, anthropology, and organization theory is Douglas, *How Institutions Think*.

12. In his classic analysis of the human capabilities required for successful cooperation, Chester Barnard concluded that memory, imagination, thought, judgment, decision, and determination are crucial, but then reflected that "in practice, a complete analysis in these respects is hardly possible in the present stage of development of psychology." Chester I. Barnard, *The Functions of the Executive* (Cambridge, MA: Harvard University Press, 1968), p. 31.

13. J. Richard Hackman, ed., *Groups That Work (and Those That Don't)* (San Francisco: Jossey-Bass, 1990), p. 479.

14. The phrase "elusive phenomena" is taken from F. J. Roethlisberger, *The Elusive Phenomena* (Boston: Division of Research, Harvard Business School, 1977).

15. In this respect, teams are small-scale examples of what some organizational theorists have called "sociotechnical systems."

16. Leonard S. Reich, *The Making of American Industrial Research* (Cambridge: Cambridge University Press, 1985), pp. 7–8.

17. The distinction between *know-how* and *know-why* is made briefly in Kim B. Clark, "Managing Technology in International Competition: The Case of Product Development in Response to Foreign Entry," in *International Com-*

petitiveness, A. Michael Spence and Heather A. Hazard, eds. (Cambridge, MA: Ballinger, 1988), pp. 39–40.

18. For example, see Hackman, ed., *Groups That Work (and Those That Don't)*, pp. 479–504.

19. The study is Augustus Abbey, *Technological Innovation* (Ann Arbor, MI: University of Michigan Research Press, 1982). The quotation appears on p. 17.

20. See William G. Ouchi, "Markets, Bureaucracies, and Clans," *Administrative Science Quarterly* (March 1980), p. 137.

21. Nathan Rosenberg and Claudio Frischtak, *International Technology Transfer: Concepts, Measures, and Comparisons* (New York: Praeger, 1985), p. vii.

22. For a detailed argument that team productivity is the "essence of the organization that we call the firm," see Arman A. Alchian and Harold Demsetz, "Production, Information Costs, and Economic Organization," *American Economic Review* (December 1972), pp. 777–795. The authors conceptualize the firm as a *"team* use of inputs and a centralized position of some party in the contractual arrangements of *all* other inputs." The quotations appear on pp. 777 and 778, respectively.

23. Hiroyuki Itami, *Mobilizing Invisible Assets* (Cambridge, MA: Harvard University Press, 1987), p. 161.

24. See Richard M. Cyert and James G. March, *A Behavioral Theory of the Firm* (Englewood Cliffs, NJ: Prentice-Hall, 1963), pp. 44–60.

25. Nelson and Winter, *An Evolutionary Theory of Economic Change*, pp. 99–107.

26. Ibid., p. 105.

27. Barnard, *The Functions of the Executive*, pp. 224–225.

28. Herbert A. Simon, *Administrative Behavior* (New York: Free Press, 1945), p. 292.

29. Kenneth J. Arrow, *Information and Economic Behavior* (Stockholm: Federation of Swedish Industries, 1973), pp. 19–23.

30. See Williamson, *The Economic Institutions of Capitalism*, Chapters 2 and 9.

31. The task of a leader, for Selznick, was building a social community with a distinctive competence by infusing an organization "with value beyond the technical requirements of the task at hand." "It is the task of leadership," he wrote, "in embodying purpose, to fit the aims of the organization to the spontaneous interests of the groups within it, and conversely to buying parochial group egotism to larger loyalties and aspirations." See Philip Selznick, *Leadership in Administration* (New York: Harper & Row, 1957), pp. 93–94. Other versions of this concept are "organizational capabilities" and "core competencies." See, respectively, Alfred D. Chandler, Jr., *Scale and Scope* (Cambridge, MA: Harvard University Press, 1990), pp. 595–597; and C. K. Prahalad and Gary Hamel, "The Core Competence of the Corporation," *Harvard Business Review* (May–June 1990), pp. 80–91.

170

170 THE KNOWLEDGE LINK

32. Akira Goto, "Business Groups in a Market Economy," *European Economic Review* (Fall 1982), p. 55.

33. This account of the Toyota production system is based on interviews with Toyota executives, March 1987; Michael A. Cusumano, *The Japanese Automobile Industry* (Cambridge, MA: Council on East Asian Studies, Harvard University, 1985), pp. 262–306; Japan Management Association, *Kanban: Just-in-Time at Toyota* (Stamford, CT: Productivity Press, 1985); and Yasuhiro Monden, *Toyota Production System* (Atlanta, GA: Industrial Engineering and Management Press, 1983). See also Koichi Shimokawa, "Japan's *Keiretsu* System: The Case of the Automobile Industry," *Japanese Economic Studies* (Summer 1985), pp. 3–31.

34. Supplier relations such as Toyota's are not peculiar to Japan. Sears, for example, has for decades followed similar practices with many of its suppliers. The economics literature of the United States and Western Europe has characterized such relationships as "partial integration" and as "vertical quasi-integration." See M. A. Adelman, "The Large Firm and Its Suppliers," *Review of Economics and Statistics*, vol. 31 (1949), pp. 113–118; K. J. Blois, "Quasi-Integration as a Mechanism for Controlling External Dependencies," *Management Decision*, vol. 18, no. 1 (1975), pp. 55–63; K. J. Blois, "Vertical Quasi-Integration," *Journal of Industrial Economics* (July 1972), pp. 253–272; and Keith MacMillan and David Farmer, "The Boundaries of the Firm," *The Journal of Industrial Economics* (March 1979), pp. 277–285. These authors assess the phenomenon mainly in terms of power.

Another view, drawing upon transactions cost economics and agency theory, is Benjamin Klein, Robert A. Crawford, and Armen A. Alchian, "Vertical Integration, Appropriable Quasi-rents and the Competitive Contracting Process," *Bell Journal of Economics* (October 1978), pp. 297–326. They argue that the structure of relationships between suppliers and buyers depends on the costs of contracting, the costs of vertical integration, and the need for both parties to find satisfactory ways to avert the opportunistic appropriation of the quasi-rents that transactions between buyers and suppliers may create.

35. Toyota's dealings with its suppliers have not been based entirely on sweetness and light. The Fair Trade Commission of the Japanese government and its Small and Medium Enterprises Agency have protected subcontractors from abuses of the kanban system. In the 1970s, Toyota changed many of its practices in response to these criticisms. See Monden, *Toyota Production System*, pp. 44–51.

36. Ibid., p. 29.

37. Ibid., p. 50.

38. These may be contrasted with "horizontal" information structures, said to be more prevalent in the United States. This economist has concluded that "the accumulation of on-the-spot knowledge as well as sharing of knowledge can be fostered only over time." This, he argues, is one of the primary reasons why the Japanese tend to emphasize long-term relations such as "lifetime"

employment and stable relational contracts with subcontractors. Masahiko Aoki, "Horizontal versus Vertical Information Structure of the Firm," *American Economic Review* (December 1986), p. 981.

39. Richard E. Caves and Masu Uekusa, "Industrial Organization in Japan," in *Asia's New Giant*, Hugh Patrick and Henry Rosovsky, eds. (Washington: Brookings Institution, 1976), p. 495. Large, powerful business groups, like the Japanese keiretsu, are also found in Mexico, Colombia, India, the Philippines, and many other countries. For an overview, see Harry W. Strachan, *Family and Other Business Groups in Economic Development* (New York: Praeger, 1976).

40. The classic study of the zaibatsu, the large Japanese conglomerates that evolved into one form of keiretsu, is Eleanor M. Hadley, *Antitrust in Japan* (Princeton, NJ: Princeton University Press, 1970), and Thomas A. Bisson, *Zaibatsu Dissolution in Japan* (Berkeley, CA: University of California Press, 1954). Other works include Caves and Uekusa, *Industrial Organization in Japan*; Cusumano, *The Japanese Automobile Industry*; and Shimokawa, "Japan's *Keiretsu* System: The Case of the Automobile Industry." Other recent studies of collaboration among keiretsu members include Ken'ichi Imai, "Japan's Industrial Organization," *Japanese Economic Studies* (Summer 1978), pp. 3–67; Akira Goto, "Business Groups in a Market Economy," *European Economic Review*, no. 19 (1982), pp. 53–70; and Yusaku Futatsugi, *Japanese Enterprise Groups* (Tokyo: School of Business Administration, Kobe University, 1976), pp. 1–101.

Complex relationships have linked Japanese firms with government agencies as well as firms outside industrial groups. For example, Japan's industrial policy linked its important firms with the Ministry of Finance, the Economic Planning Agency, and the Ministry of International Trade and Industry. In the 1950s and 1960s, the agencies intervened actively in decision making and financing at important firms. From 1978 to 1988, as the firms grew more successful and powerful, and as Japan acceded to international pressures to liberalize its economy, the "strong" forms of industrial policy yielded to subtler, gentler ways of harmonizing company decisions with the government's economic goals. Finally, Japanese banks and insurance companies—through keiretsu arrangements—not only lend large sums to Japanese firms but are permanent shareholders in them.

A recent systematic and comprehensive comparison of Japanese industrial practices with those of the United States is Thomas K. McCraw, ed., *America vs. Japan* (Boston: Harvard Business School Press, 1986). More specialized works include Chalmers Johnson, *MITI and the Japanese Miracle* (Stanford, CA: Stanford University Press, 1982) on the history of Japanese industrial policy from the 1920s to the 1980s; James C. Abegglen and George Stalk, *Kaisha* (New York: Basic Books, 1985) on the competitive strategies and practices of Japanese firms; and Andreas R. Prindl, *Japanese Finance* (New York: John Wiley, 1991) on links among firms within the Japanese financial system. Japanese industrial relations are described in detail in Japan Institute of Labor, *The Japanese Employment System* (Tokyo: Japan Institute of Labor, 1980), and in Taishiro Shirai, ed., *Contemporary Industrial Relations in Japan* (Madison, WI: University of Wisconsin Press, 1983).

41. The history of Mitsui, up to the late 1960s, is presented in rich detail in John G. Roberts, *Mitsui: Three Centuries of Japanese Business* (New York: Weatherhill, 1973).

42. For an overview of contemporary theoretical perspectives on the groups, see Masahiko Aoki, *Economic Analysis of the Japanese Firm* (New York: Elsevier Science Publishers, 1984). Their role in the Japanese economy in the decades just after the Meiji Restoration is summarized succinctly in Keiichiro Nakagawa, "Business Strategy and Industrial Structure in Pre-World War II Japan," in *Strategy and Structure of Big Business*, Keiichiro Nakagawa, ed. (Tokyo: University of Tokyo Press, 1975), pp. 3–38. The economic effects of these groups on their members are analyzed in Caves and Uekusa, "Industrial Organization," and in Richard E. Caves and Masu Uekusa, *Asia's New Giant* (Washington, DC: The Brookings Institution, 1976). They conclude that group membership, in general, lowers rather than raises member firms' return on equity and return on assets. Another interpretation of the group's economic role is Iwao Nakatani, "The Economic Role of Financial Corporate Grouping," in *Economic Analysis of the Japanese Firm*, Masahiko Aoki, ed., pp. 227–258. Nakatani characterizes the groups as vast "implicit mutual insurance schemes" whose profits are lower than those of independent firms because of the benefits the groups provide to their executives, workers, and shareholders. Because some of the benefits— wages, dividends, and interest payments—reduce profits, they account for the group's weaker financial performance. For Nakatani, however, the group's role is not profit maximization but using its monopoly power to service joint utility of its constituents, particularly, employees, stockholders, financial institutions, and management. Some Japanese scholars have extended this argument further, concluding that Japanese capitalism has "collapsed" because large Japanese businesses are run by "management workers" whose aim is "the perpetuation of the firm as a communal body." The pursuit of profits is simply a means for achieving this objective, and for assuring that all workers, including "management workers," have satisfactory, secure, and satisfying livelihoods. See also Tadanori Nishiyama, "The Structure of Managerial Control: Who Owns and Controls Japanese Businesses?," *Japan Economic Studies* (Fall 1982), pp. 37–77.

43. Michael Y. Yoshino and Thomas B. Lifson, *The Invisible Link* (Cambridge, MA: MIT Press, 1986), p. 6.

44. Ibid., pp. 198, 199, 213.

45. In the words of another study:

> The large sogo shoshas do regular monitoring of the technological environment of all major western nations, and much

of this data is linked on line to corporate headquarters in Tokyo
and Osaka. Major foreign cities like London, New York, and
Frankfurt are the base of a beehive of intelligent sourcing from
technical magazines, trade journals, company reports, and government studies . . . all foreign markets and technological trends
which are then supplemented by detailed company studies.

See Charles J. McMillan, *The Japanese Industrial System* (New York: Walter
de Gruyter, 1984), pp. 103–104.

46. Goto, "Business Groups in a Market Economy," p. 55.

47. Everett M. Rogers and Judith K. Larson, *Silicon Valley Fever* (New York:
Basic Books, 1984), p. 79.

48. Ibid., p. 80.

49. Other such communities are described in Michael J. Piori and Charles F.
Sabel, *The Second Industrial Division* (New York: Basic Books, 1984),
pp. 28–54. Where does this line of reasoning—which starts with the premise
that some knowledge and capabilities are rooted primarily in relationships—
ultimately lead? In all likelihood, it reached its speculative apogee in the writings
of the French Jesuit and paleontologist Pierre Teihard de Chardin. In 1925,
he coined the term "noösphere" to refer to the totality of all human knowledge
and values, all the human minds in which they exist, and all the links among
human beings. In the words of the English biologist Sir Julian Huxley, the
noösphere is the "sphere of mind" enveloping the earth, which de Chardin
believed was evolving toward a union of all human beings into what Huxley
calls a "single interthinking group based on a single self-developing framework
of thought.

   Sir Julian Huxley's introduction to Teilhard de Chardin's *The Phenomenon of Man* attempts to make precise the term "noösphere," even though
de Chardin did not define it explicitly. See Pierre Teilhard de Chardin, *The
Phenomenon of Man* (New York: Harper & Brothers, 1959), pp. 11–28.

50. Michael E. Porter, *The Competitive Advantage of Nations* (New York:
Free Press, 1990), p. 151.

51. See Kenneth J. Arrow, *Essays in the Theory of Risk-Bearing* (Chicago:
University of Chicago Press, 1971), p. 74.

52. The difficulties of transferring knowledge through market relationships are
discussed in detail in David J. Teece, "The Market for Know-How and the
Efficient International Transfer of Technology," *Annals of the American Academy of Political and Social Science* (November 1981), pp. 81–96. In addition
to the "paradox of information," Teece stresses the difficulties of controlling or
appropriating know-how after a bargain has been struck and of actually implementing the transfer. Broader analyses of the strengths and weaknesses of markets
as instruments of communication are Thomas Sowell, *Knowledge and Decisions*
(New York: Basic Books, 1980), and Oliver E. Williamson, *The Economic
Institutions of Capitalism* (New York: Free Press, 1985), especially pp. 292–

294. See also Mark Casson, *The Firm and the Market* (Cambridge, MA: MIT Press, 1987), pp. 121–153.
53. This example is based upon the analysis of the relationship between GM and Fisher Body in the 1920s as described in Benjamin Klein, Robert G. Crawford, and Armen A. Alchian, "Vertical Integration, Appropriable Rents, and the Competitive Contracting Process," *The Bell Journal of Law and Economics*, vol. 21 (October 1978), pp. 297–326.
54. A sketch of such roadways appears in "Boulevard of Dreams," *The Economist*, September 24, 1988, pp. 113–114.
55. They were Burroughs, Sperry, NCR, Control Data, and Honeywell.

Chapter 5

1. Paul B. Carroll, "IBM Joins With Siemens AG," *The Wall Street Journal*, January 25, 1990, p. B4.
2. Michael Polanyi, *Personal Knowledge: Towards a Post-Critical Philosophy* (Chicago: University of Chicago Press, 1948), p. 53.
3. This description of Fanuc and GMF Robotics is based upon an interview with Eric Mittelstadt, president and CEO of GMF Robotics, November 1987; Fanuc Annual Reports, 1983–1987; Kuni Sadamoto, *Robots in the Japanese Economy* (Tokyo: Survey Japan, 1981); Centre for Business Research, *The World Market for Industrial Robots* (Manchester, England: Centre for Business Research, 1986); Shinichi Kamata, "GM-Fanuc Joint Venture Will Build Robot Factory in Michigan," *Japan Economic Journal*, May 3, 1983, p. 10; "Next-Century Car Builder," *American Metal Market/Metalworking News*, February 3, 1986, pp. s8–s10; and Gene Bylinsky, "Japan's Robot King Wins Again," *Fortune*, May 25, 1987, pp. 53–58.
4. Ideally, a preemptive strategy secures several important advantages and not just one. The move is difficult for competitors to copy; it exploits rivals' weaknesses; it builds upon the firm's strengths; and the preempting firm can reverse its move, if necessary. Through its relationships, GM aimed to seize advantages across the full range of critical activities in the auto industry: supplier relations, product design, basic research, manufacturing systems, customer relations, and distribution in service. An analytic overview of preemptive strategies is Ian C. MacMillan, "Preemptive Strategies," *The Journal of Business Strategy* (Fall 1985), pp. 16–26.
5. Niccolo Machiavelli, *The Prince*, translated by George Bull (London: Penguin Books, 1981), p. 51.
6. An operating system is a collection of software that assists and in part controls a computer's basic operations. It coordinates the reading and writing of data between the internal memory and such peripheral devices as disk drives, keyboards, and printers; it also prepares the computer to execute applications programs.

7. This overview of AT&T and its computer efforts is based on Charles P. Lecht, "The Waves of Change," *Computer World*, May 30, 1977, pp. 11–13; David A. Loehing, "Ma Bell vs. IBM?," *Barron's*, February 9, 1976, pp. 3, 14, 16, 22; Michael A. Verespej, "Clash of the Titans," *Industry Week*, May 27, 1985, pp. 64–68; Richard Brandt and John W. Verity, "Unix: The Soul of a Lot of New Machines," *BusinessWeek*, March 14, 1988, pp. 94–96; Brenton R. Schlender, "AT&T, Sun, Looking to Open Windows of Opportunity," *The Wall Street Journal*, April 11, 1988, p. 6; and Jonathan B. Levin, "Will Sun Melt the Software Barrier?," *BusinessWeek*, April 18, 1988, p. 72.

8. This account of IBM Japan's efforts in telecommunications is based on interviews with IBM Japan executives and on "NTT Signs Pacts with IBM," *Electronic News*, March 4, 1985, p. 40; "Mitsubishi's New Communication Adviser Lays Plans for Data Services," *Data Communications*, March 1984, pp. 115–116; and Carla Rapoport, "NTT, IBM Japan Agree Software Systems Venture," *The Financial Times*, September 26, 1985, p. 4.

9. Howard Anderson, "The IBM-MCI Merger: An Evaluation," *Telecommunication Products and Technology* (August 1985), pp. 21–25; and Frances Seghers, "Now If MCI Can Just Keep the Party Going," *BusinessWeek*, May 16, 1988, p. 39.

10. This overview of IBM's efforts in software and systems integration is based on interviews with IBM executives; "Computer Industry Trend: System Integration," *Nikkei Computer*, April 1, 1988, pp. 42–58; Edith Myers, "Risk and Responsibility," *Computer World*, November 18, 1987, pp. 43–45; Paul Gaskell, "Alien Connection," *Systems International* (September 1987), pp. 35–37; "IBM, Mitsubishi Bank in Software Effort," *Electronic News*, October 19, 1987, pp. 12, 20; Peter Freeman, "Software Development Systems," *Computers and People* (September–October 1987), pp. 11–27; and "Nissan and IBM Japan Agree to Jointly Set Up New Company," press release, IBM Japan, January 14, 1987.

11. For an extended and critical assessment of IBM's long-term prospects in telecommunications, see Richard T. DeLamarter, *Big Blue: IBM's Use and Abuse of Power* (New York: Dodd Mead, 1986), Chapter 5.

12. The overview of Saturn's technology and systems is based on an interview with Richard LeFauve, President, Saturn Corporation, October 5, 1988; personal communications with GM managers John Barry DuVall and William McPherson; "Till the Magic Goes," *Manufacturing Systems* (September 1986), pp. 32–36; Bryan H. Berry, "It's Now or Never for World-Class Auto Making at GM," *Iron Age*, November 7, 1986, pp. 34A1–35; Dale D. Buss and Melinda G. Guiles, "GM Slows Big Drive for Saturn to Produce Small Car in Five Years," *The Wall Street Journal*, October 30, 1986, p. 1; and "Saturn: It's on Target for '90 Introduction," *Automotive News*, April 25, 1988, pp. 1, 64.

13. Roger B. Smith, "A New Age of Almost Cosmic Industrial Achievement," *The Journal of Business Strategy* (March 1984), p. 80.

14. Anne B. Fisher, "Behind the Hype at GM's Saturn," *Fortune*, November 11, 1985, p. 44.

15. David Whiteside, "How GM's Saturn Could Run Rings Around Old-Style Car Makers," *BusinessWeek*, January 28, 1985, p. 126.

16. "Developments in Industrial Relations," *Monthly Labor Review* (October 1985), p. 49.

17. Stewart Brand, *The Media Lab* (New York: Viking, 1987), pp. 1–16.

18. See Michael E. Porter, *The Competitive Advantage of Nations* (New York: Free Press, 1990), pp. 152–165.

Chapter 6

1. This chapter draws heavily on more than 30 interviews I conducted with managers involved in the joint activities of GM and IBM. In these, I discussed lessons they had drawn from their experience managing alliances.

        In addition, the chapter draws on Raymond Vernon, *Sovereignty at Bay* (New York: Basic Books, 1972); John M. Stopford and Louis T. Wells, Jr., *Managing the Multinational Enterprise: The Organization of the Firm and Ownership of the Subsidiaries* (New York: Basic Books, 1972); Lawrence G. Franko, *Joint Venture Survival in Multinational Corporations* (New York: Praeger, 1973); Farok J. Contractor and Peter Lorange, *Cooperative Strategies in International Business*, (Lexington, MA: Lexington Books, 1987), pp. 253–369; Kathryn Rudie Harrigan, *Strategies for Joint Ventures* (Lexington, MA: D. C. Heath, 1985), pp. 355–375; and Benjamin Gomes-Casseres, "Multinational Ownership Strategies," unpublished Ph.D. diss., Harvard Business School, Boston, 1985.

2. A comprehensive framework for thinking through these issues appears in C. K. Prahalad and Gary Hamel, "The Core Competence of the Corporation," *Harvard Business Review* (May–June 1990), pp. 79–91.

3. A persuasive argument that the balance of benefits in relationships often changes, not as a result of perfidy, but because of harder work, better business judgment, and superior strategy by one of the partners, is found in Gary Hamel, Yves L. Doz, and C. K. Prahalad, "Collaborate with Your Competitor—and Win," *Harvard Business Review* (January–February 1989), pp. 113–139.

4. For evidence that firms have often followed this precept, see Benjamin Gomes-Casseres, "Joint Ventures in the Face of Global Competition," *Sloan Management Review* (Spring 1989), pp. 17–26.

5. The role of a gatekeeper is described in detail in Hamel, Doz, and Prahalad, "Collaborate with Your Competitors—and Win," pp. 136–139.

6. Studies of joint ventures corroborate many of these concerns. For example, two scholars concluded that:

> Long overseas experience on the part of a firm goes hand in hand with the preference for wholly owned subsidiaries over joint ven-

> tures (and a preference for any kind of subsidiary over a li-
> cense). . . . where an effective strategy demands that the firm
> should be able to exercise a high degree of control over its foreign
> affiliates, the presence of other parties participating in the direction
> of the affiliate will be counted as a negative factor.

See Raymond Vernon and Louis T. Wells, Jr., *The Manager in the International Economy* (Englewood Cliffs, NJ: Prentice-Hall, 1986), p. 64. A recent study of 35 North American and Western European joint ventures, in contrasting them with internal efforts, concluded that "joint ventures are a much more difficult form of organization to manage well." See J. Peter Killing, *Strategies for Joint Venture Success* (New York: Praeger, 1983), pp. 8–12.

Another study, this one of joint ventures between U.S. and Japanese companies in the 1960s and 1970s, led its authors to conclude that "the joint venture has always been an awkward compromise of conflicting interests." See James C. Abegglen and George C. Stalk, *Kaisha* (New York: Basic Books, 1985), pp. 226–231. A McKinsey & Company study concluded that of all the firms that started out with some general intention of creating a partnership with another firm, only about 2% eventually created an arrangement that proved to be a long-term success. Of course, many of them did not proceed with their initial concept, and others, who could not find a suitable partner with whom to do business, were never able to test their concept. But even in the cases where two firms signed a formal agreement, only one in three lasted beyond the lifetime of the product lines involved in the partnerships. See Norm Alster, "Dealbusters: Why Partnerships Fail," *Electronic Business*, April 1, 1986, p. 72. George Taucher, a professor of business administration at IMEDE in Switzerland, has concluded even more pessimistically that "strategic alliances are doomed." He gives four basic reasons for his view: firms' shifting strategies, the sheer complexity of many alliances, lack of a clear decision-making focus, and career considerations that create conflicts between the goals of the alliance and the self-interests of the managers involved. See George Taucher, "Beyond Alliances," *IMEDE: Perspectives for Managers*, no. 1, 1988.

7. Killing, *Strategies for Joint Venture Success*, p. 84.

8. Managers use other terms, such as credibility, a sense of personal obligation, commitment, mutual respect, a capacity for listening and understanding—a family of precepts closely related to trust and open communication. In a similar vein, the author of a recent study of 35 joint ventures in North America and Western Europe observed that:

> If you ask parent company personnel about the success
> of their joint ventures, in nine of ten answers the idea of a trust
> will figure prominently. The following comment . . . is quite typi-
> cal: "So far, we have enjoyed very successful experiences with all

> our foreign partners. Profits and growth in the environment of trust
> and mutual respect have been the gold rules of our relationship."

See Killing, *Strategies for Joint Venture Success*, p. 82. Evidence for the importance of trust also comes from studies of the factors that contributed to successful cooperative endeavors such as joint ventures. See also Sol E. Flick, "The Human Side of Overseas Joint Ventures," *Management Review* (January 1972), p. 29; Mark Zimmerman, *How to Do Business with the Japanese* (New York: Random House, 1985); Richard W. Wright, "Joint Venture Problems in Japan," *Columbia Journal of World Business* (Spring 1979), pp. 25–31.

Even in the United States, with its reputation for individualism and litigiousness, there is evidence that many important economic activities are governed mainly by informal, private arrangements based on trust and confidence. See, for example, Stewart Macaulay, "Non-Contractual Relations in Business: A Preliminary Study," *American Sociological Review* (Spring 1963), pp. 55–67. Macaulay concluded that "businessmen often prefer to rely on 'a man's word' in a brief letter, a handshake, or 'common honesty and decency'—even when the transaction involved exposure to serious risk." Even when two companies did use a contract to specify formally their relationship, Macaulay found that legal sanctions were rarely used to make adjustments when subsequent events made adjustments necessary. One executive who participated in this study said, "You can settle any dispute if you keep the lawyers and the accountants out of it. They just do not understand the give and take needed in business." (Ibid., p. 61.)

9. For a detailed analysis of this observation about joint ventures, see Killing, *Strategies for Joint Venture Success*, pp. 82–85.

10. This description of the organization of GM's activities in Japan is based on interviews with GM personnel at the General Motors Overseas Corporation in Tokyo and in Detroit, and on internal documents they provided.

11. The study, by James P. Wonrock, is cited in Maryann Keller, *Rude Awakening* (New York: William Morrow, 1989), p. 134.

12. Michael F. Wolff, "Technology Transfer: A GM Manager's Strategy," *Research-Technology Management* (September/October 1989), pp. 9–10.

Chapter 7

1. GM was not a citadel, in my sense of the term, throughout all of its history. In the first decades of this century, under the management of its founder, William Durant, GM was a loose confederation of automobile makers, component manufacturers, and other companies. Even after Alfred Sloan's reorganization in the 1920s, it held minority stakes in a number of firms such as Bendix Aviation. But nearly all of these equity positions had been sold by the

early 1950s, and the government ordered Du Pont to sell its large holdings of GM stock in 1956. It was then that GM evolved into what I have termed a citadel.

2. "General Motors' Position on United Control of Foreign Operations," General Motors Corporation, February 11, 1966, p. 3.

3. "Saab and GM Both Benefit from 50-50 Deal," *Automotive News*, December 18, 1989, pp. 1, 47.

4. Samuel Perry, "IBM and Siemens to Cooperate on 64-Megabit Chip," Reuter Business Report, January 24, 1990.

5. Joseph B. White, "GM's Opel Unit Forms a Venture in East Germany," *The Wall Street Journal*, April 16, 1990, p. B6.

6. David Stipp, "Soviets to Develop Technology in West in Joint Venture with Arthur D. Little," *The Wall Street Journal*, February 22, 1990, p. B2.

7. "Window Shopping," *The Economist*, February 17, 1990, p. 75.

8. Orville J. McDiarmid, "Japan and Israel," *Finance and Development* (June 1966), p. 136.

9. J. H. Plumb, *The Italian Renaissance* (New York: American Heritage, 1985), p. 34.

10. Peter F. Drucker, "The Coming of the New Organization," *Harvard Business Review* (January–February 1988), p. 47.

11. Karl Polanyi, *The Great Transformation* (Boston: Beacon Press, 1965), pp. 48–55, 68–75; and Joseph A. Schumpeter, *Capitalism, Socialism, and Democracy* (New York: Harper & Row, 1975), pp. 150–155.

INDEX

Index